Exploration: A Very Short Introduction

VERY SHORT INTRODUCTIONS are for anyone wanting a stimulating and accessible way into a new subject. They are written by experts and have been translated into more than 40 different languages.

The series began in 1995 and now covers a wide variety of topics in every discipline. The VSI library now contains more than 400 volumes—a Very Short Introduction to everything from Indian philosophy to psychology and American History—and continues to grow in every subject area.

Very Short Introductions available now:

Available soon:

For more information visit our website

www.oup.com/vsi/

Stewart A. Weaver

EXPLORATION

A Very Short Introduction

OXFORD
UNIVERSITY PRESS

OXFORD
UNIVERSITY PRESS

Oxford University Press is a department of the
University of Oxford. It furthers the University's objective
of excellence in research, scholarship, and education
by publishing worldwide.

Oxford   New York

Auckland   Cape Town   Dar es Salaam   Hong Kong   Karachi
Kuala Lumpur   Madrid   Melbourne   Mexico City   Nairobi
New Delhi   Shanghai   Taipei   Toronto

With offices in

Argentina   Austria   Brazil   Chile   Czech Republic   France   Greece
Guatemala   Hungary   Italy   Japan   Poland   Portugal   Singapore
South Korea   Switzerland   Thailand   Turkey   Ukraine   Vietnam

Oxford is a registered trade mark of Oxford University Press
in the UK and certain other countries.

Published in the United States of America by
Oxford University Press
198 Madison Avenue, New York, NY 10016

Library of Congress Cataloging-in-Publication Data
Weaver, Stewart Angas
Exploration : a very short Introduction / Stewart A. Weaver.
pages   cm—(Very short introductions)
Includes bibliographical references and index.
ISBN 978-0-19-994695-2 (paperback)
1. Discoveries in geography—History.
2. Explorers—History.   I. Title.
G80.W34   2014
910.9—dc23   2014016789

Printed by Integrated Books International, United States of America
on acid-free paper

For Tanya

Contents

List of illustrations

Preface

Books about exploration tend toward either the encyclopedic or the monographic. With a few notable exceptions, they aspire either to lengthy and lavishly illustrated coverage of everything or to detailed, close examination of something. This book, in keeping with the general purposes of the *Very Short Introduction* series, aspires to neither. Rather, by way of a few carefully chosen episodes in the history of exploration, it offers a broad, thematic overview of the subject as a whole. After an opening effort at a definition of exploration in several aspects, it proceeds chronologically but unevenly through the ages, telling some familiar stories in what I hope will be unfamiliar ways. My purpose throughout has been to put the work of exploration in the context of its time. Exploration may be (as explorers themselves like to say) a timeless aspect of the human condition: we wander as if by instinct. But like any cultural endeavor it also bends to the spirit of each age, and in the chapters that follow I have tried to show how. Behind almost every sentence lies a dauntingly large body of literature, very little of which I have alluded to directly. I encourage anyone wanting more to refer to the bibliographic outline at the book's end or simply to undertake further explorations of their own.

For various sorts of help and encouragement along the way, allow me to thank Nancy Toff and Rebecca Hecht at Oxford University Press; the anonymous reviewers of my proposal and manuscript; my children, Cea and Henry Weaver; my stepchildren, Dasha and Sophia Lynch; and above all my wife, Tatyana Bakhmetyeva.

Chapter 1
What is (and is not) exploration?

Strictly speaking, *exploration* is the noun form of the English verb *to explore*, meaning (as the *Oxford English Dictionary* has it) "to investigate, seek to ascertain or find out," to "look into closely," or "to search into or examine [a place] by going through it; to go into or range over for the purpose of discovery." The honor of the earliest recorded usage of the verb goes to Queen Elizabeth I, who in an admonitory letter of 1585 to her royal cousin James VI of Scotland, refers to various "baiting stratagems...by sondry meanes to be explored." But the noun is a little older, first appearing in a 1543 Act of Parliament that tells how Sir William Bowyer, knight and mayor of the City of London, in an effort to remedy the city's failing water supply had "by diligent search and exploration founde out dyuers greatte and plentyfull sprynges at Hampstead heath." Elizabeth's usage is figurative: we retain it today every time we speak of *exploring every possibility* or *exploring a subject further*. But in her father's Act of Parliament, with its passing reference to Sir William Bowyer's purposeful wanderings across the wilds of Hampstead Heath, we have something like our modern literal understanding of *exploration*. The first definition in *Encarta Webster's Dictionary of the English Language* is "travel for discovery," that is, "travel undertaken to discover what a place is like or where it is."

Travel for discovery: one could hardly ask for a more succinct or serviceable definition of *exploration* at the outset. This book offers a very short introduction to exploration—not in the general sense of inquiry or examination into a subject but in the specific spatial and historical sense of travel and discovery. But even thus specifically defined, exploration remains an expansive and elusive category of human experience, one that finds full meaning only in juxtaposed distinction to closely related but ultimately different things. Explorers travel, yes. But so do nomads, migrants, pilgrims, traders, vagrants, and vacationers. The line between these forms of travel is never fully fixed: many a trading mission, many a pilgrimage has involved untold feats of exploration. The defining difference lies in the sense of purpose. Both the trader and the pilgrim ultimately seek a known even if remote and exotic destination; they do not self-consciously travel to find something new. The explorer, on the other hand, by definition has no fixed or certain destination. The point of his or her journey is to see what has never been seen before, to cross over previously untraveled ground.

Thus the customary emphasis in discussions of exploration on the collateral category of discovery: travel for the sake of discovery. But if closely related, so closely as often to appear interchangeable, exploration and discovery are not the same thing and rest on opposite theoretical assumptions. Discovery is an event: it assumes a world of facts or places waiting to be found, collected, classified, and it signifies a summation, a climax, a final moment of truth or revelation. Exploration, on the other hand, is a contingent process, an open-ended activity that however planned or programmed ultimately unfolds spontaneously in active engagement with the unknown or unfamiliar. The discoverer arrives, the explorer wanders. The discoverer finds, the explorer seeks. One can explore without discovering anything at all, just as one can discover by accident, without exploring anything at all. Historically, however, the two experiences often go together and lend each other potency. It is an exploring mentality that makes discoveries significant rather than happenstance, intellectual rather than randomly factual. And exploration usually justifies itself by way of discovery. Exploration leads to discovery. A true explorer is a traveler who seeks a discovery.

But what does discovery mean in a geographical context? As critics of Eurocentric accounts of exploration are always quick to point out, most of the world had already been settled or indigenously occupied for thousands of years before any intrepid westerner set out to "explore" it. But for the unapproachable wastelands of polar ice or desert sand, almost everything had been seen before; almost all terrain had been previously traveled by some anonymous someone. In what sense can Christopher Columbus, then, to take the classic case, be said to have discovered anything at all, given that the Caribbean islands he accidentally happened upon in 1492 were already home to as many as two million Taino Indians?

1. "Perhaps we ought to ask the chaps over there whether *they've* ever discovered it." A 1975 cartoonist's perspective on the ambiguous status of "discovery" in a fully inhabited world.

In no sense, some would say. Columbus discovered nothing. Yet if we take *discover* in its archaic but literal sense to mean uncover, reveal, or expose—if by *discover* we mean something more like disclose, then Columbus's title as a great discoverer begins to have more warrant. He was not the first to see or travel through the Caribbean archipelago. But he was the first to disclose its existence to those who had not known of it, the first to get to it from somewhere else and, even more importantly, return to describe it to those back home. No one can deny the indigenous claim to prior occupation of the Americas. But to insist on a prior Native American discovery of America is, as one of Columbus's most fair-minded biographers has said, to miss the point that discovery is not a matter of being in a place but of getting to it, of establishing routes of access from somewhere else, and then returning to spread the news of it abroad. Discovery in this sense assumes the end of cultural isolation, as does exploration. Exploration is news. To qualify as an explorer, one must not only find something new but write about it, publicize it, draw the attention of others to it. Explorers are not the first to experience the places they describe; they are the first to describe them to people of their own kind, the first from a particular culture, says the *Oxford Book of Exploration*, to encounter and experience new lands and people, and then disclose their existence to those back home.

Disclosure alone, however, will not end cultural isolation and will not make for thoroughgoing discovery unless it leads to sustained contact of decisive cultural consequence. Why is Leif Eiriksson, the Norse explorer who indisputably reached the New World roughly five hundred years before Columbus set sail from Lisbon, not generally reckoned to have "discovered" America? By rights he should be: though inspired by an earlier chance sighting of land in the west by his countryman Bjarni Herjolfsson, Leif had no known destination in mind when he set out across the North Atlantic from Greenland in the year 1001. He sought something new, found it, briefly occupied it, and then returned home to tell others about it. His North American landfall was exciting news that inspired others to follow in his wake, and though not immediately celebrated in print as Columbus's landfall was, it lingered long enough in Icelandic folk memory to be captured and immortalized in two great sagas—the *Greenlanders' Saga* (ca. 1200) and *Eirík's Saga* (ca. 1210–30)—some two hundred years after the fact. In no sense, then, ought the Norse discovery of America to be discredited. It may have begun accidentally with Bjarni Herjolfsson's being blown off course en route from Norway to Greenland, but it continued in a genuinely exploratory spirit and led incontrovertibly at L'Anse aux Meadows, Newfoundland, to the first attempt at a permanent European settlement in the Americas.

Sadly for Leif Eiriksson's ultimate standing as an explorer, his landfall in North America did not lead to a decisive or permanent change in the way Europeans generally pictured or inhabited the world. His was a happenstance discovery that left no legacy outside of Norse folk memory, once the fledgling settlements themselves had been abandoned at some point in the eleventh century. Columbus, on the other hand, left an enormous, world-altering legacy. The transatlantic routes he pioneered and the voyages he publicized decisively altered European conceptions of global geography; in addition, they led almost immediately to the European colonial occupation of the Americas and thus permanently joined together formerly distinct peoples, cultures, and biological ecosystems. The specific consequences that flowed from the permanent Columbian contact of 1492 (as opposed to the fleeting Norse contact of 1001) are many and momentous. The general point is that exploration in the fullest sense leads to cultural convergence. It is a critical part, the catalytic part of that long-term historical process by which cultural isolation has broken down and the world become essentially one.

In this process of cultural convergence, travel alone, though certainly requisite, is less decisive than the acquisition and dissemination of new knowledge. But "new" in this context did not always mean accurate, rational, or observably true. Indeed, one paradoxical effect of European exploration in the much-vaunted Age of Discovery was to revive many of the elements of what Joseph Conrad once derided as "Geography Fabulous." He was speaking here of the medieval cartographic tendency to indulge "circumstantially extravagant speculation" and crowd the blank spaces of the map "with pictures of strange pageants, strange trees, strange beasts, drawn with amazing precision in the midst of theoretically conceived continents." The more people knew, the more they imagined; the more informed, the more credulous they became.

Columbus himself is an exemplary case here, insofar as his seemingly rational choice of a westward route to the Indies turned into a bizarre and arcane quest for the terrestrial paradise. Later, with the advent of the Scientific Revolution and the Enlightenment, exploration would lose to some extent this Janus face—there would be no chasing after mythic will-o'-the wisps for James Cook, whose very purpose was to replace such lingering earthly illusions as the great southern continent of Terra Australis or the fabled Northwest Passage with precisely observed and minutely surveyed reality. But it never lost it entirely. Exploration by its very nature tends toward exaggeration, and even today the line between an explorer's report and a traveler's tale is not always easily fixed.

For the essence of exploration, some would say, is not the acquisition of knowledge but rather adventure, another closely aligned category of human experience. The very words "exploration" and "discovery" are often elided in the popular imagination with "adventure," as much of the centennial acclaim surrounding the polar exploits of Robert Scott, Roald Amundsen, and Ernest Shackleton, for instance, suggests. But however adventurous in aspect, exploration should never be reduced to adventure, to dramatic feats of derring-do by outsized (either heroic or eccentric) individuals who in the face of the world's scorn and nature's fury win through to claim a great virgin prize or (better yet) die trying. Explorers, no less than artists, poets, soldiers, or statesmen, are representative people of their time and, more often than not, exploration—far from expressing an eccentric wandering urge on the part of some rugged visionary—is the outward projection of cultural imperatives shaped and elaborated back home. Meriwether Lewis and William Clark were doubtlessly men "of courage undaunted," as Thomas Jefferson said. But too exclusive an emphasis on the adventurous details of their overland trip still tends to obscure one critical aspect of their famous expedition, namely the extent to which it was planned in advance by Jefferson and his scientific associates back home. In one aspect at least, Lewis and Clark were less the rugged individualists of legend than the trained agents of a civilized culture when they set out into the wilderness on the leading edge of American westward expansion.

No amount of planning or training can anticipate the vagaries of the wilderness, however. If in the popular imagination explorers too often come across simply as men and women of undaunted courage and indomitable will, in the scholarly (or at least academic) imagination they too often come across simply as the blunt instruments of empire, as so many human missiles of Europe thoughtlessly aimed and fired into the peripheral void. Exploration in practice inevitably involves a good deal of improvisation—something a missile cannot manage—and here both adventure and wayward purpose will often emerge, along with a surprising degree of cross-cultural accommodation to local circumstance.

Take for example the eminent case of Alexander von Humboldt, the Prussian geographer, naturalist, and explorer whose five-year expedition through Latin America between 1799 and 1804 sustained a long lifetime's work at the cosmic intersection of the physical, biological, and anthropological sciences. Widely celebrated in his own day as the "Nestor of scientific travelers," a "second Columbus," one of those rare "wonders of the world," as Emerson said, "who appear from time to time, as if to show us the possibilities of the human mind," Humboldt subsequently fell into near-total obscurity as a Darwinian insistence on the struggle for existence eclipsed his more benign vision of a harmonious cosmic order and as the age of the enlightened polymath gave way to that of the tightly disciplined specialist.

But if largely forgotten, Humboldt was never actively reviled until the 1980s, when postcolonial theory came of age and found in him a perfect instance of the explorer as oppressor. However dressed up it may have been in the innocent terms of romantic science, Humboldt's true purpose (so the argument goes) was the ideological recasting of South America in the service of European empire. The effect of his travel writing was to reduce South America to pure nature, drain it of any prior human presence or history, and thus lay it open to rampant exploitation and abuse. Never mind that Humboldt consistently attacked Spanish misrule in his published writings or that he confided to his journal that "the very idea of a Colony is immoral." As an explorer beholden to the Spanish crown for access to the jungle, he was inevitably an instrument of colonial domination, an arrogant racialist who assumed a godlike, omniscient stance over the planet in order to subdue it and appropriate it to European systems of knowledge and control.

Such interpretations as this one are common wherever the history of European (especially) exploration is concerned, and they have much to recommend them, especially as correctives to a traditional emphasis on valorous and disinterested discovery. However motivated, exploration is always intrusive, and it often leads to violence, conquest, enslavement, or even extermination. But to emphasize the fatal impact exclusively, as postcolonial criticism tends to do, is mistakenly to position a dynamic and invulnerable European culture against a static and wholly vulnerable indigenous one. In fact it is to accept the very binary

8

distinction between European society and tribal culture
on which the whole colonial enterprise was founded in the
first place.

It is also to overlook the extent to which almost without exception
western explorers relied on the active assistance and collaboration
of native peoples who often had their own independent purposes
in mind. We need to move beyond fixed binary distinctions and
consider the active and fluid nature of the explorer's experience.
Explorers made it up as they went along. As necessarily threshold
figures placed at the point of original contact between worlds, they
often had a flexible and culturally syncretic way of responding to
situations that the word "imperial" cannot encompass. As people
of their time, they no doubt tended to see what they were
conditioned to see. But exploration is always surprising; it defeats
expectations, challenges certainties, even opens eyes from time to
time. And in Humboldt's case, as those who have read him fully
and fairly have found, it led to ambivalence at the very least where
empire was concerned and to genuine humility before the glory
of creation and the wonder of planet Earth.

The same could not be said of such a figure as Henry Morton
Stanley, the Welsh-born journalist and African adventurer whose
preference for what his critics called "exploration by warfare"
obviously emerged from colonial arrogance and the new imperial
will to power. But even he relied on collaborative relationships
with African tribesmen to an extent that undermined colonial
assumptions and belied the foundational racial premise that
the white man was always in charge. The nineteenth-century
exploration of Africa was a two-sided and symbiotic process
involving both Europeans and Africans in a host of leading,
following, and mediating capacities. Far from being the passive
objects of the imperial gaze, Africans were active agents in the
exploration of their own homelands. They gazed back and
imposed on the often weak and vulnerable European explorer
their own sets of purposes and ambitions.

Thus when Richard Burton and John Hanning Speke set out to explore the lake regions of Central Africa, they did so not under the Union Jack but under the red flag of Zanzibar. And so complete was David Livingstone's dependence on the indigenous Makololo when he undertook his celebrated sub-Saharan crossing of Africa in 1854 that he was arguably leading an African expedition under the authority of an African ruler. Explorers loved to talk about "blanks on the map," as if the continents were empty and uncharted seas, but what they found, more often than not, were communities of people on whom they had to rely for their survival. Thus the consistent and irreconcilable tension between exploration as imagined and exploration as experienced. Long defined in terms of discovery of the unknown, exploration (at least of the world's inhabited spaces) is really about encounter and cultural contact. It is about what happens "on the beach," when one world meets another and two hitherto separate stories become one.

Sadly, from the point of view of the historian of exploration, one party to the beach encounter left little on record about it. We have thousands of pages worth of the journals of Captain James Cook; we have almost nothing directly from the Polynesian islanders whose lives intersected with those of him and his men in the course of three momentous voyages. But we have more indirectly than we once knew. By attending closely to both the presence in the text of the native islanders and to the hard-won insights of cultural anthropologists, one can in fact render Pacific exploration not as the story of the "fatal impact" of one culture on another but rather as an intricate drama of mutual discovery, of exploration on two sides. Cook was a great explorer, as the traditional story holds. But so was Tupaia, the Tahitian high priest and navigator who guided Cook on his first voyage through the vast expanse of the Central Pacific and mediated his every encounter with indigenous island peoples before dying of a fever at journey's end in Batavia (today's Jakarta). Almost every western explorer, at one time or another, had a Tupaia, a native guide, interpreter, intercessor.

With the prominent exception of Lewis's and Clark's revered Sacajawea, the guide seldom makes it into the popularly received version of expedition lore. But he (Tupaia) or she (Sacajawea) nevertheless embodies what exploration is often fundamentally about: mediation, intercession, cultural negotiation, and sometimes, even, symbiosis.

In the long run, though, for all the effort at mutual discovery and two-sided understanding, and despite the individual explorer's own ambivalence and vulnerability, exploration usually encouraged some form of occupation, conquest, or control. With few exceptions, wherever explorers went, trade or faith or industry or empire followed—thus their obvious significance to the making of the modern global world. No mere adventurers or renegade travelers, explorers were the forgers of links, the spinners of webs. They were the primary agents of contact not just between cultures and peoples but between whole ecosystems and environments. To that joint anthropological and ecological extent, exploration ultimately means *change*: it is a particularly adventurous form of original travel involving discovery, cultural contact, and change.

But when did it begin? Who were the first explorers?

Chapter 2
The peopling of the earth

When historians speak of "the Age of Exploration" they usually mean the period beginning in the mid-fifteenth century, when a potent combination of commercial, cultural, and technological circumstances first took Europeans across the high seas in sufficient numbers to claim and occupy what they found. Pride of place in this familiar story goes to the Portuguese or, even more particularly, to the fifteenth-century Portuguese prince known as Henry the Navigator, who from his castle atop the "Sacred Promontory" of Sagres at the very southwestern extremity of Europe, allegedly presided over his country's first forays into the North Atlantic. Despite having never once embarked on a voyage of exploration himself, Prince Henry thus often figures as the essential impresario of modern exploration, one whose faith in his own destiny and zeal for the unknown somehow epitomizes the exploring turn of mind. But no one would ever call Henry the first explorer. People have lived on this planet a very long time, and wherever they have lived, they have wandered. The first explorer, one might reasonably imagine, was that nameless hominid who somewhere around a million and a half years ago led a few of his or her kind away from the East African tree where man was born and off into the vast and empty horizon.

Out of Africa

The deep origins of exploration are inseparable from the long process of the peopling of the earth that began between one and two million years ago, with the migration of *Homo erectus* out of the rift valleys of eastern Africa and proceeded by fits and starts across the ages until roughly the fourth millennium BCE, by which time most of the inhabitable world had been at least sparsely settled. Whether this long global dispersal of, first, *Homo erectus*, and then of our more direct ancestor, *Homo sapiens*, should qualify as exploration is open to question. For one thing, the dispersal was completely anonymous: it left no textual record of any kind—a serious disqualification among those for whom exploration assumes a written report, one that alters other people's perceptions of the world around them. For another, it probably did not reflect a conscious urge to open up the world to view; it did not involve exploration for exploration's sake. Rather, as far as paleo-anthropologists can tell, the peopling of the earth reflected the simpler primitive urge toward survival. *Homo sapiens* migrated in response to changing climatic conditions and in search of food, security, and safety—gathering and foraging as they went but not in any deliberate sense exploring.

On the other hand, one among many possible etymologies of the word explore traces it to the Latin *explorare*, meaning (as some dictionaries have it) "to cry out, as to rouse game." If this is fair, then *Homo sapiens*, the "wise human" becomes almost synonymous with *Homo explorans*, the "human as explorer." Subsistence migration becomes, in essence, exploration. Moreover, ethno-archaeologists now generally believe that hominid societies relied on small and relatively mobile parties of advance scouts both to forage for food and to establish the likeliest routes of seasonal migration. What is advance scouting if not travel for the sake of discovery, if not the formation of new knowledge in continuous passage through space? The written record is still missing, along with direct evidence of world-altering cultural encounter. But scouting implies a report of some kind: it is most definitely *news*. It is not about being in a place but getting to it *and* returning to lead others there. To that extent at least, in these nameless hominid scouts we have the world's earliest explorers.

Unlike their modern counterparts, these first explorers were agents of cultural dispersal. They did not bring people together; they drew them apart. They did not make the world smaller; in leading people away from their place of common origin, they made it larger by way of geographical separation and cultural isolation. Of course there must have been episodes of contact along the way. Even in the earliest times, some routes of subsistence migration must have intersected. And insofar as the territories behind the lead migrants tended to fill up with settlers and nomads, humans were not really drawing apart as their global reach expanded. Still, in trying to identify a dominant pattern in the long sweep of past time, historians have lately found it useful to think in terms of a long period of dispersal and divergence, during which migrating peoples settled in their own remote corners of the earth and developed their own distinctive cultures, languages, technologies, and faiths in isolation from one another, and then a much shorter period of drawing together, mutual rediscovery, contact, and cultural exchange.

Just when this grand tide turned, when the human story turned from one of continual partings to one of continual meetings is difficult to say with any precision. Some suggest roughly 1000 CE—more or less the moment, not coincidentally, of Norse contact with aboriginal North Americans. But dating aside for now, the conceptual point is that history has two such stories to tell—one of divergence and one of convergence—and that both are stories of exploration.

The first story, that of continual partings, defies easy or uncontroversial summary. The best genetic and archaeological evidence has human beings out of Africa and in the Middle East somewhere between 100,000 and 70,000 years ago. All extra-African people descend from these first wanderer-explorers, who repeatedly parted company as they made their way first south and east into Asia, and then, some 40,000 years ago, north and west into Europe, where they either displaced or killed off the archaic remnants of Neanderthal man. Helped by low-lying sea levels, the peopling of the earth proceeded mostly by easily traversed land, but the original settlement of Australia between 45,000 and 60,000 years ago, when it was already separated by at least fifty miles from mainland Asia, must have relied on a primitive form of nautical technology and thus suggests a genuine exploring mentality. Just when and how people first arrived in the Americas is a subject of fierce, often politically motivated debate. The emerging scholarly consensus suggests an original foot migration from eastern Siberia across the land bridge of Beringia about 12,000 years ago. And with that, with the late-Pleistocene settlement of North and South America and (from about 2500 BCE) Greenland, the peopling of the earth was largely complete. Of the currently inhabited world, only Austronesia (including Oceanic Polynesia and Madagascar) and Iceland then remained empty, two great standing challenges to two of history's greatest exploring peoples: the seafaring Polynesians and those Norse voyagers often known to history as the Vikings.

The sea people of the west

Where did all the people come from? For the better part of ten years, on three separate voyages, Captain James Cook, the greatest explorer-navigator of his age, had been roaming the vast expanse of the South Pacific, and everywhere he went, on every island he "discovered," he found people, or they found him. Cook was not a man easily given to astonishment, but on January 30, 1778, as he sailed away from his first sojourn in the Hawai'ian Archipelago, he could not help wondering how such a dispersal of seemingly homogeneous people ever came to happen. "How shall we account for this Nation spreading it self so far over this Vast ocean?" he asked himself in his journal. "We find them from New Zealand to the South, to these islands in the North and from Easter Island to the [New] Hebrides; an extent of 60° of latitude or twelve hundred leagues north and south and 83° of longitude or sixteen hundred and sixty leagues east and west, how much farther is not known, but we may safely conclude that they extend to the west beyond the [New] Hebrides."

How could this be? One traditional answer traceable to Álvaro de Mendaña's sighting of the inhabited Marquesas group in 1595 was that the Pacific islanders must have come from a nearby southern continent, from the great antipodal land that European science presumed to exist as a necessary earthly counterweight to the continental landmasses of the north. But by the time he got to Hawai'i in 1778, Cook had laid the myth of the Great South Land to rest, and remembering how the natives of Tahiti and Tonga had often outsailed his tri-masted ships in their double-hulled canoes, his first instinct was to credit purposeful, long-range Polynesian seamanship. European prejudice would ultimately not allow for savage mastery of the sea, and by the time he came to write up the narrative of his third voyage, Cook had evidently changed his mind and decided that the "detached parts of the earth" must have been peopled by accident, by waifs and strays driven far off their short chosen courses by adverse winds and currents. The prevailing wind in the South Pacific is easterly—that is, it blows from east to west. Any notion that the Polynesian islanders might have migrated deliberately from the East Asian mainland or Melanesia against the prevailing wind seemed on the face of it improbable. So, after Cook, the idea took hold that they must have been blown there accidentally by rogue westerlies and that Polynesia was thus in essence a kingdom of castaways.

One theoretical alternative was that Polynesia had been settled downwind from the east, that is, from South America—a sensational notion that the Norwegian explorer Thor Heyerdahl sought to bolster when he sailed his balsa raft *Kon-Tiki* along the Humboldt Current from Callou, Peru, to the Tuamotu islands in French Polynesia in 1947. But little archaeological or anthropological evidence confirms the theory of an eastern origin, and the more prosaic notion of accidental "drift voyaging" from the west hung on until the 1960s, when a generation of scholars relatively unblinkered by European colonial prejudice and skilled, some of them, in the largely lost art of celestial navigation, began to look soberly and scientifically into the related questions of when, how, and why the ancient Polynesians might have purposefully set their simple sails to the outermost ends of the earth.

And what they found was the most adventurous episode of exploratory migration in all of human history. For some 40,000 years, the Austronesian descendants of the original Pleistocene settlers of western Melanesia—New Guinea, the Bismarck Archipelago, the Solomon Islands—had clung to the edges of the Great Ocean, fishing and farming, but also staring out to sea while exploring the reefs and lagoons that made up such a distinctive part of their intercoastal world. Then, sometime around 6,000 years ago, after who knows how many halting attempts, they climbed into their *va'a tauna*, their double-hulled voyaging craft and took off into the wind. Yes, into the wind, or at least at a reasonable angle to it, for that way they assured themselves of safe return: a crucially defining feature of successful exploration. Counterintuitive though it sounds, historically almost all maritime exploration has proceeded into the wind, for the simple reason, again, that only this method allows for trial and error, for reconnaissance and retreat, for wayfinding and safe return to tell others how to follow.

The Austronesians hit on this upwind innovation and suddenly reached out across 720 miles of open sea to the island clusters of Samoa, Tonga, and Fiji. Here they paused again and established the distinctive island culture that archaeologists call *Lapita*, after the site in New Caledonia where they first found the distinctive red earthenware characteristic of Near Oceania. This was already impressive enough: the dispersal of *Lapita* pottery throughout the Bismarck Archipelago, Vanuatu, New Caledonia, Fiji, and Samoa proves the existence of a long-range trade that could only have been sustained through adventure voyaging. But what followed was more impressive still, when, sometime around the year zero of the Common Era (give or take three hundred years), they set out both westward to Madagascar and eastward across 4,000 miles of open sea to what they called Fenua'enata and the Spanish later called the Marquesas.

By any reasonable standard, this first voyage in a *va'a tauna* from some unknown beach in Samoa or Tonga, probably, across the vast expanse of the South Pacific to the Marquesas was arguably the most remarkable voyage of discovery and settlement in all of history. That it might have happened by reckless or accidental drift voyaging on adverse or unseasonable winds is not just improbable; it is virtually impossible. Decades of close analysis of South Pacific wind patterns combined with both computer-simulated and authentically reenacted voyages has shown as much and thus made the case for deliberate, directed navigation preceded by a period of careful and systematic exploration.

They would have begun modestly, these first Polynesian migrants, heading their free-sailed and double-hulled canoes first close into and then across the wind, probing, penetrating, feeling their way farther each time into the sea before turning downwind for home and safety to report on what they had or had not found. They had neither compass nor clock nor sextant nor telescope nor any of the tools of modern, scientific navigation. What they had in abundance was generations' worth of accumulated knowledge of the look and feel of the sea and the sky, and so they paddled and sailed by intuitive dead reckoning in a way that instrument-dependent Europeans could neither comprehend nor admire. And when they were ready, when the lead explorers were reasonably confident of what they would find, they loaded the hulls and connecting deck of the *va'a tauna* with perhaps as many as eighty people and 65,000 pounds of precious cargo (including domesticated animals and plants), and set off for a new life into the sunrise.

2. Hawai'ian artist Herb Kawainui Kāne's speculative rendering of *va'a tauna*, the ancient Polynesian voyaging canoe, is based on a petroglyph found at Orongo on Rapa Nui (Easter Island).

Why they did so is now the more difficult question for archaeologists and anthropologists to answer than how. Mainly, it seems, population growth in the homeland of Samoa and Tonga had put a strain on resources and limited the subsistence and status opportunities for all but first-born sons. And so the later-born left for the oldest of migrants' reasons: to seek a better life. But warfare and exile and the casting out of the shamed or defeated may have been involved as well, along with simple wanderlust and the explorer's joy of discovery. Polynesian folklore retains the legend of Hina-fa'auru-va'a (Hina-the-canoe-pilot), who once having explored all the earth with her brother Ru, set off for the moon in her canoe *Te-apori* and was never seen again—a living suggestion, perhaps, of the leading role that women may have played in Polynesian exploration. Unlike Hina, however, most Polynesians came home from their wanderings, at least in the early years of the migration. Archaeological evidence suggests not just deliberate but also repeated, two-way, out-and-back voyaging— another essential marker of a true culture of exploration.

The chronology of the Polynesian migration, precisely when these great seafarers went where, is endlessly contested, though radiocarbon dating makes the broad outlines reasonably clear. A few centuries after the first voyage to the Marquesas, sometime between 400 and 800 CE, the *Enata*, as they called themselves, turned restless again and undertook another great settlement voyage to Hawai'i at the northern fringe of "the Polynesian Triangle." One hundred years later, give or take a few, they daringly crossed 2,200 miles of open sea to Rapa Nui (Easter Island), the loneliest spot on the globe and the eastern limit of their settlement migration. Shortly thereafter, sometime between 800 and 1000 CE, they turned southwest from their original homeland to Aotearoa, to New Zealand. And with that, with the fixing of the third extreme point of the Polynesian Triangle, they were done. A remarkable thousand-year burst of exploratory oceanic migration was, but for the missing island bits in between, essentially complete.

Or was it? In 1991 archaeologists working on Mangaia, the most southerly of the Cook Islands in Central Polynesia, found the carbonized remains of a prehistoric sweet potato—a humble enough find, one might think, except that the sweet potato is an American domesticate that could have gotten to Polynesia only if someone had brought it there. Eleven years later, archaeologists digging at the prehistoric El Arenal site in Chile found a chicken bone that predated the Spanish presence and thus, by the same nonindigenous logic, could have gotten to America only if someone else had brought it there. These and subsequent similar findings, together with the increasingly sophisticated results of simulated and experimental sailings, have recently revived and lent powerful new credence to an old idea: that sometime in the late Holocene era—between 700 and 1350 CE, probably—Polynesian seafarers landed in the Americas in places extending from Chile to southern California. Thor Heyerdahl had it backwards, it turns out. Americans did not sail to Polynesia. Polynesians sailed to America, where, for the first time in all their wanderings, they made contact with other people, specifically at the very least the Mapuche people of south-central Chile. They did not stay long, establish colonies, or alter the course of New World history in any way. But in this humble exchange of a chicken for a potato, we have evidence of both fleeting cultural contact and a great (if anonymous) feat of transoceanic exploration, one that possibly led some centuries before Columbus to the first maritime discovery of the Americas.

The Norse Atlantic saga

Unless of course the Vikings got there first. However intriguing, the possibility of a Polynesian landfall in the Americas remains somewhat speculative and, at best, imprecisely dated. The Norse landfall, on the other hand, has been definitively proven and radiocarbon dated to precisely the turn of the first millennium, 997 CE, probably, plus or minus eight years. The place was L'Anse aux Meadows, a windswept headland overlooking the Strait of

Belle Isle at the northernmost tip of Newfoundland. And however unimposing a place—to date, the remains of nine small buildings have been found—however lightly or briefly occupied it may have been, it has an enduring and incontrovertible significance as the first authentic and universally accepted site of European settlement in the New World. Pending further discoveries elsewhere, it also represents the far western extremity of a great folk migration, one that like the roughly simultaneous Polynesian migration would have required stunning feats of maritime exploration.

In the case of the Norse, however—*Norse*, for the northern Scandinavian seafarers who happened on Newfoundland were not the raiders and plunderers of Viking legend—we know the names of the people involved, a simple fact that secures for them a firmer place in the highly individualized annals of exploration. We also have written sources that describe the feats involved—inconsistent literary sources, to be sure, most of them dating to a century or two after the fact. But scholars point to the surprising durability of Norse oral tradition and argue that there is as much fact as fancy in the sagas that describe the settlement of Greenland, for instance. With the Norse, the peopling of the earth leaves the realm of the purely anthro-archaeological and enters that of the ethno-historical. It leaves a flesh-and-blood story to tell.

Conventionally, the story might begin with the Viking raid on the Northumbrian monastery of Lindisfarne in 793 CE, or with founding of Dublin under Olaf the White in 841, or with the Varangian settlement of the old Russian towns of Staraya Ladoga and Novgorod in 862, or with the Norse occupation of Iceland in 874. The point is that this first transatlantic migration was part of a much larger story of Scandinavian expansion in all directions from the late eighth through the tenth centuries. The causes of this general expansion were just what one would expect: demographic pressure and land shortage at home, resentments over local misrule, the ever-widening impulse toward trade and the finding of better things in life, restlessness, curiosity, the desire for fortune and fame. Only here and there and now and then did the migration involve the kinds of pillage and plunder we classically associate with the Viking age. Early-medieval Scandinavians were in general farmers and fishermen. They were looking for good land where they could settle their families and supplement their meager agricultural livelihoods with fish, game, and a modest trade in simple surplus goods.

To the south and east such strivings called for little in the way of exploration: the travel routes were well established, the lands already settled and occupied. But to the west lay the unknown waters of the North Atlantic, and here the exploring genius of the Norse came into its own. Their boat, for this ocean-going purpose, was not the dragon-headed longship of Viking-age cliché but the broader and sturdier *knarr*—a clinker-built trading vessel, essentially, with decking fore and aft, an open cargo hold, and a firmly seated mast for one large, square-rigged, coarse woolen sail. Steered by rudder from the starboard quarter and equipped with oars for coastal maneuvering, the *knarr* was a strong, versatile, ship of all work. But compared with the Polynesian *va'a tauna*, it did not sail well into the wind, and so the Norse proved the daring exception to the general rule of maritime exploration. They did not explore upwind but down, taking advantage of the East Greenland Current to carry them from the Norwegian Sea to the Labrador Sea, from Europe to America.

It sounds bold and reckless, and brave it certainly was. But the Norse were no more spendthrift of life than the Polynesians, and their way across the Atlantic conformed cautiously to the classic principle of Norse navigation: to make the shortest practicable passage using the clearest visible landmarks. Lacking compass and chart, they sailed by dead reckoning, fixing their latitude by nautical instinct and the help of a bearing dial—a handheld wooden disk with a central peg designed to cast the sun's noontime shadow. They risked much by sailing with the current

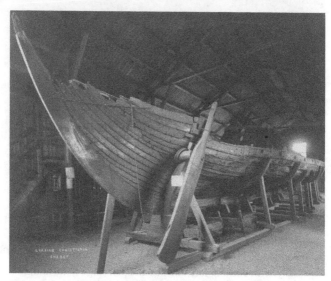

3. A nineteenth-century photograph of the Gokstad Viking ship. Built around 850 CE and found in a Norse burial mound in Sandefjord, Norway, in 1879, the Gokstad is a seventy-six-foot clinker-built longship that might have been used for raids, trade, and voyages of exploration around the time of the Norse settlement of Iceland.

downwind, and so, not surprisingly, compared with the Polynesians before them or Columbus after, they were modest shore-huggers whose maritime achievement lay in a distinctive mix of accidental, wind-blown sightings and planned voyages of exploration. They generally knew roughly where they were going, insofar as they understood the earth's sphericity and thus were reasonably sure of hitting something sometime. And given the speed of their ships—a fully laden *knarr* might have managed 120 miles or more in a day—and the coastal topography of the North Atlantic, they would never have been out of sight of land for very long. In good weather, the crossing from Iceland to Greenland, for instance, would have taken about four days.

Moreover, initially at least, the Norse Atlantic explorers were following in the wake of Irish anchorite monks who had already lightly—very lightly—settled the Faeroe Islands and Iceland at some point in the mid-to-late eighth century. Their inspiration was St. Brendan the Navigator, the wandering Irish abbot who according to medieval legend set off westward from the Dingle Peninsula for the Promised Land of the Saints in a plank-built rowboat at some point in the early sixth century. The notion that he somehow wound up in Newfoundland instead is a hagiographic and nationalist fiction—one of many such to mark the popular chronicles of exploration. But Brendan was nevertheless a real person who probably made real sea journeys to the Orkneys and Shetlands sometime before his death around 570 or 580 CE. And his alleged landfall on the "Isle of the Blessed" or "St. Brendan's Isle"—somewhere off in the heart of the North Atlantic—truly captured the imagination of later explorers, Christopher Columbus notably among them. Meanwhile, his example encouraged those astonishingly brave penitential monks who in an effort to emulate the isolation of John the Baptist abandoned themselves to wind and current in their fisherman's curraghs and wound up, some lucky few of them, in Iceland.

Converging on the North Atlantic as they did from both Scandinavia and the British Isles, and in particular Ireland, the Norse had very likely picked up rumors of Iceland before they half went looking for it and half stumbled on it sometime in the mid-ninth century. According to tradition as preserved in the thirteenth-century *Landnámabók* or *Book of the Settlements*, the actual discoverer was Naddod the Viking whose storm-driven ship missed the Faeroe Islands and made accidental landfall at Reydarfjord in the Eastfirths in about 860. Serious exploration followed under Flóki Vilgerdarson (who, noticing the glacial floes in the northwestern fjords, bestowed the name "Iceland" on the place) and then serious settlement starting at Reykjavik in the southwest and proceeding clockwise around the island, coast by coast, until all the good land had been claimed and occupied by about four hundred leading families. Diverse sources tell the story somewhat differently, but the tripartite pattern of accidental sighting, followed by deliberate exploration, followed by attempted occupation is always the same. And it significantly repeats itself twice over, in Greenland and America.

In the case of Greenland, an accidental storm-tossed sighting of small islands off the eastern coast by Gunnibiorn Ulf-Krákasson in about 900 CE led to a three-year sustained exploration by the twice-banished outlaw Eirík Rauda Thorvaldsson ("Eirík the Red") beginning in 982. From a landfall at Bláserk on the inhospitable east coast, Eirík made his way south around Cape Farewell and then up the deeply fjorded southwest coast to what became the future sites of Norse settlement. Precisely how far north up the Davis Strait Eirík ventured over the subsequent two summers is unclear: some think he went as far as Disco Island at latitude 70°. But even setting that uncertain possibility aside, the distances involved in his first exploration of Greenland add up to at least 3,300 miles of open sea and another 1,000 miles in the inner fjords. By any measure this was one of the most impressive feats of travel and discovery ever known.

Once established in Greenland—Eirík returned with a colonization fleet in 984—the Norse were bound to hit on North America before long. Just north of the Arctic Circle near present-day Sisimiut (Holsteinsborg), the Davis Strait separating Greenland from Baffin Island, Canada, narrows to about two hundred miles. Hunters working north out of the Western Settlement near present-day Nuuk (Gothåb) might well have *seen* North America before anyone sailed to it, and recent archaeological evidence suggests the possibility of a Norse presence on Baffin Island up to one hundred years before the confirmed settlement of L'Anse aux Meadows. The traditional literary evidence speaks to a first accidental sighting in about 985, when Bjarni Herjolfsson drifted off his course for Greenland in a thick fog and came upon unknown lands to the west. He did not explore them himself, but his subsequent report caused a great stir back in Norway and in Greenland, and "there was now great talk of discovering new countries," as the *Greenlanders' Saga* pithily puts it—good evidence, if any were needed, of a true culture of exploration. By this time, Eirík the Red's sailing days were behind him, and so it fell to his son Leif to undertake the exploration of the lands Bjarni had sighted and to establish the first European foothold on American shores.

How long it lasted and indeed what particular purpose it served are matters of unending debate. Some see L'Anse aux Meadows as a way station between the Norse settlements in Greenland and another larger, as yet undiscovered settlement on the Gulf of St. Lawrence to the south. Others see it as a mere overwintering camp for parties from Greenland and a base for limited exploration of the Newfoundland region. Either way, despite the flights of popular fancy that would place the Vikings as far south as Florida and as far west as Minnesota, it marks the approximate limit of Norse territorial expansion and the apex of their exploring ambitions.

It is also the place where the peopling of the earth came finally to a close, the place where two human populations migrating around the world in opposite directions met each other for the first time. The Norse had found Iceland empty but for a few Irish hermits— *Papar*, they called them—whose existence the archaeological record has yet to confirm. Greenland had long been home to a succession of pre-Inuit, Paleo-Eskimo, and Late Dorset peoples, but these had all withdrawn from the south before the Norse arrived, and the archaeological record suggests only the most limited, occasional, and fleeting contact, if indeed any. It was only in Newfoundland or thereabouts that the Norse encountered full on those whom they called "skrælings," the ancestors, probably, of the Mi'kmaqs of New Brunswick, the Beothuks of Newfoundland, or the Montaignais of southern Labrador. Whatever their precise identity, the aboriginal peoples whom the Norse met and evidently failed to overawe—thus their quick departure from American shores—were in the vanguard of the great human migration that had turned east out of Africa into central Asia and Siberia and, ultimately, North America. The Norse were in the vanguard of those who had turned west for Europe. And in Newfoundland, at the westernmost margin of Norse maritime exploration, the two vanguards met, the global circle of humanity closed, and the first of history's two big stories, that of human divergence, ended, and the second, that of human convergence, began.

Chapter 3
First forays

To say that history's second big story began with the Norse encounter with aboriginal Americans in Newfoundland is, in two respects, too dramatic. For one, the Norse did not persist in their American adventure anymore than the Polynesians persisted in theirs. By all accounts, the settlement at L'Anse aux Meadows lasted fewer than twenty-five years. Those in Greenland lasted far longer and may have served as bases for fur-and-timber-gathering forays to North America until sometime in the fourteenth century. But with their final abandonment around 1450, the Norse Atlantic saga came to a close without having either ended American isolation or altered European geographical thinking. For all their nautical prowess and demonstrable appetite for exploration, the Norse had somehow reached America and even settled there for a while without ever consciously discovering it. They were the brief custodians of a North Atlantic outpost of Europe whose contact with America and with Native Americans made no deep or lasting impression on either.

Moreover, though the Norse may have achieved the first "full circle" contact with humans migrating around the earth in the opposite direction, they cannot really be said to have initiated human convergence per se. The world's far-flung peoples had been coming back together in less globally circumferential ways for a long, long time, often at the backs of notable explorers whose routes proved more enduring and culturally significant than those of either the Polynesians or the Norse. As long ago as 2270 BCE, for instance, a governor of Upper Egypt named Harkhuf undertook the first of his four expeditions up the Nile River at the command of Pharaoh Merene, who was eager to extend his rule southward into Nubia (today's Sudan). Sometimes celebrated as "the first known explorer," Harkhuf was one of many ancient Egyptian travelers who had pioneered a lasting mesh of commercial trade routes along the upper Nile, around the Red Sea, and through the eastern Mediterranean by the middle of the second millennium BCE.

A century or so later, the Levantine people known to history as the Phoenicians, having already established maritime colonies in the western Mediterranean, came to the Pillars of Hercules flanking the Strait of Gibraltar and decided to sail on through, thus becoming the first of the world's people's to brave the waters of the Atlantic. How far they ventured north along the Iberian coast and south along the Moroccan in their search for tin and murex—the precious dye-excreting mollusk that lent the color purple to ancient imperial authority—is unclear: perhaps as far north as Brittany and Cornwall, as far south as Agadir. They were not explorers for exploration's sake and so did not sail west into the open ocean at all. Even so, simply by running the Strait of Gibraltar they dispelled a great fear and set a lasting precedent for those Mediterranean sailors who would one day venture farther.

Ancient anticipations

Ancient exploration faintly enters the historical record around 500 BCE, when according to his own barely surviving account Hanno the Navigator, nominal king of Carthage, reconnoitered the northwestern coast of Africa as far south as Senegal and perhaps farther. In his famous *Naturalis Historia* (77–79 CE), the Roman writer Pliny the Elder alludes further to one Himilco, a Carthaginian contemporary of Hanno, who allegedly sailed into the deep Atlantic as far as the equatorial Doldrums, but Himilco's own account is lost, and given the fabulous elements of the story as it comes down to us, complete with sea monsters and mid-ocean shallows, few scholars give it much credit.

More confident accounts of ancient exploration begin with Pytheas of Massalia, a Greek geographer and mariner who sometime around 325 BCE sailed north out of the Bay of Biscay and did not stop until he had rounded the coast of Brittany, crossed the English Channel, and fully circumnavigated "the islands of Pretanni," that is, the British Isles. Neither merchant nor soldier, Pytheas was evidently an independent adventurer and disinterested scientific traveler—the first, for instance, to associate ocean tides with the moon. Whether he made it as far north as Iceland as some like to think (based on his reference to "the land of Thule") is doubtful, but he somehow knew of the midnight sun, and he evidently encountered arctic ice. Even conservative estimates give him credit for some 7,500 miles of ocean travel—an astounding feat for the time and one that justifies Pytheas's vague reputation as the archetypal maritime explorer. He did not contribute to cultural convergence in any decisive way, but as a traveler of uncommon audacity, courage, curiosity, and skill who also thought to keep a record of his travels, he somehow anticipates from an ancient distance the great age of exploration to come.

Meanwhile, the eastern conquests of Pytheas's princely contemporary, Alexander the Great of Macedon, had fatefully introduced the Greeks and the entire Hellenistic world to the luxurious allurements of Arabia and India. Toward the end of his Indian campaign in 324 BCE, Alexander, as much explorer as conqueror, descended the Indus River to its mouth near present-day Karachi, from where he dispatched a fleet under Nearchus of Crete to explore some 1,400 miles of unknown coast westward back to Babylon. He thus put the Arabian Sea on Greek maps for the first time and before his death in 323 sent further expeditions to reconnoiter both the Red Sea and Persian Gulf routes to India. Unknown Indian seafarers were meanwhile reconnoitering in the opposite direction, helping to make the Arabian Peninsula an early point of cultural contact between the South Asian subcontinent and Mediterranean Europe.

China remained largely a world apart until at some remotely unspecified time the Chinese themselves began to dispatch trade caravans westward along what came eventually to be called the Silk Road—the overland route from China through Central Asia to the Levant and, ultimately, the Mediterranean. Here, the recorded explorer of note was Zhang Qian, a sort of roving ambassador of the Han emperor who in 139 BCE set out from Chang'an (modern Xi'an) for the Hellenistic kingdom of Bactria, where he hoped to recruit soldiers for the emperor's war on the nomadic Xiongnu people. In diplomatic terms, Zhang Qian's twelve-year mission proved a complete failure, insofar as he returned home without a single recruit to the emperor's cause. But his journey across the formidable Pamirs into Transoxiana as far as Samarkand in today's Uzbekistan and then back via Tibet stands as one of the great achievements of ancient exploration, and one that contributed decisively to cultural convergence. In short, Zhang Qian opened the eyes of the Chinese to a civilized world beyond their borders and provided the geographical stimulus to the further opening of the Silk Road.

Just as the campaigns of Alexander the Great had stimulated Hellenistic exploration to south and east, so the campaigns of Julius Caesar stimulated Roman exploration to the north and west. But if Caesar deserves a place in the history of exploration, it is more for his literary than his military genius: *Commentarii de Bello Gallico*, his firsthand account of the Gallic Wars from 58 to 52 BCE, included compellingly reliable accounts of the geography and peoples of Gaul and thus for the first time brought Western Europe decisively within the grasp of the Mediterranean imagination.

The most notable achievement of ancient exploration, however, was an even more purely intellectual one. So far as anyone can tell, Claudius Ptolemy, the author of the second-century treatise *Geographia*, never left his study in Alexandria, where he lived from ca. 90 to ca. 168 CE. But drawing widely and imaginatively on the knowledge of others, he both confirmed ancient understanding of the spherical character of the earth and, more importantly still, devised a method of measuring it spatially by way of coordinated degrees of latitude and longitude. Unlike his ancient predecessor Eratosthenes, he grossly underestimated the circumference of the earth, and he believed that between the westernmost point of Europe and the easternmost point of Asia lay a single intervening sea: thus the fatefully mistaken ambition, eventually, of Christopher Columbus. Still, by devising a cartographic system on which to hang geographical knowledge, Ptolemy made global exploration possible. Moreover, in rejecting the old Homeric image of a single, contiguous world surrounded by empty ocean, he suggested the possibility of vast unknown lands and so encouraged exploratory ambitions for centuries and centuries to come.

Pilgrims, merchants, and ambassadors

The arrival of Buddhism in China in or around the first century CE proved a further stimulus to overland travel a few centuries later, when a number of the Chinese faithful felt irresistibly drawn to India and its holy shrines. Of these, the earliest was Faxian (Fa Hsien), who in 399 CE set off from his home in Chang'an on foot westward across the trackless Takla Makan desert, then south across the Pamirs to the Kingdom of Peshawar in today's Pakistan, and then east into the plain of the Ganges, where he lingered for six years before making his way home by way of the Bay of Bengal, Ceylon, and Sumatra. More than two hundred years later, the great Xuanzang (Hsuan Tsang) undertook an even more epic, sixteen-year journey through much of China, Central Asia, and India (including the forbiddingly mountainous regions of Kashmir and Nepal). Faxian and Xuanzang were heroic travelers whose written memoirs have earned a deserved place in such modern anthologies as *The Oxford Book of Exploration*.

But their status as explorers is nevertheless open to some discussion, insofar as they generally followed at least vaguely established routes for well-established pilgrimage destinations. They did not self-consciously seek the new or frame their travels in terms of geographical discovery, any more than did Christian pilgrims to Jerusalem or Muslim pilgrims to Mecca in the centuries after the rise of Islam. Pilgrims are undeniably cultural ambassadors whose travels take them over difficult and sometimes unknown ground. The first walkers of El Camino de Santiago, for instance, had to hew their way through unbroken wilderness to the very end of the earth (Cape Finisterre) in northwestern Spain. But even they were explorers mostly in a spiritual sense—seekers after heavenly salvation more than earthly knowledge.

The same sorts of qualifications apply to all those pioneering missionary priests who took advantage of the *Pax Mongolica*, the century's long peace that followed the consolidation of the Mongol Empire across the Eurasian continent in the mid-thirteenth century, to travel eastward to China and the court of the Great Khan at Karakorum. The first of these, Father Giovanni de Piano Carpini, a Franciscan monk-turned-roving-envoy of Pope Innocent IV from 1245 to 1247, was the first European to leave an authentic account of the steppe-land route across Central Asia. The second, Friar William of Rubruck, was the more notable explorer of the two, however, insofar as his account of roughly the same route by way of the Caspian and Aral Seas, Lake Balkhash, and the Altai Mountains to Mongolia attended more closely than his predecessor's not just to historical and ethnographic but also to geographical and topographical detail.

Rubruck, for instance, was the first European to prove that the Caspian was an inland sea and not, as the ancients had believed, an embayment of the Arctic Ocean. But though servant of a different master—in his case King Louis IX of France—he no less than Father Giovanni was in pursuit in the first instance of diplomatic intelligence and in the second of spiritual salvation. His travel memoir, *The Journey of William of Rubruck to the Eastern Parts of the World, 1253-1255*, is now reckoned one of the great works of medieval geographical literature, but it was narrowly circulated and relatively unknown until the sixteenth century. To the history of exploration, the more important work, if only for the extent of its influence on the thinking of Christopher Columbus, is the *Description of the World*, more commonly known as *The Travels of Marco Polo*.

The author, or at least the leading co-author of this most famous of all travel books, was one Rustichello of Pisa, an Italian romance writer who sometime around 1298 found himself for obscure reasons sharing a Genoese prison cell with a middle-aged Venetian merchant who had evidently spent the better part of his life wandering the length and breadth of the known world, from the Arctic Ocean to Java and from Zanzibar to Japan. How far Marco Polo had actually traveled either on his own family's Asian trading missions or in diplomatic service to Kublai Khan and how far he relied for his knowledge, rather, on secondhand accounts picked up in Constantinople or the Black Sea ports is endlessly debated and unknown. It is also, in some sense, beside the point. Rustichello, recognizing in what he heard from his fellow prisoner the elements of a great story, worked them up with Marco's assistance into a book that became the single most powerful inspiration for the European age of exploration.

For what it lacked in geographical specificity and clarity—not one of the many manuscript and printed editions ever included something so mundane or helpful as a map—the *Travels* more than compensated with an abundance of detail about Asian life, manners, customs, and, above all, riches. Its pages teemed with exotic descriptions of the splendid cities of Cathay, of richly ornamented buildings, pleasure gardens, plentiful markets, marble palaces, and royal warehouses filled with gold, silver, and gemstones. And though obviously heightened for literary effect, it was not altogether implausible. Indeed, the real wonder of the *Travels* was how it managed to combine its fabulous allurements with an aura of rigorous authority. Fifty years after Marco Polo's death in 1324, the makers of the famous Catalan Atlas relied with some confidence on his geographical testimony in attempting the first real cartographic rendering of Asia. And Columbus of course was a true believer, especially where the vast eastward stretch of Asia was concerned and the far-too-distant placement, some 1,500 miles out from China, of the gold-gilded, pearl-encrusted island of Japan, his cherished "Cipangu."

Not that Columbus had many authorities to choose from when it came to his eastern speculations. A few Franciscan missionaries followed Marco Polo into China, including one, Giovanni da Montecorvino, who made a closer study than the Venetian merchant had of the monsoon cycle in the Indian Ocean and its bearing on the possibility of an overseas route to Cathay. But by the time of Giovanni's death in Beijing in 1328, the hold of the Great Khan over his vast Asian dominion was weakening, and forty years later, with the advent of the Ming Dynasty, it collapsed altogether. The first western mission to leave a trace in Chinese historical record, that of the Florentine Franciscan Giovanni de' Marignolli, was also the last. Under the Ming, China reverted to isolationism; the revival of Islam in the Golden Horde raised a new barrier between Asia and western Christendom; and the peculiar conditions that had made possible Europe's first great age of overland discovery expired along with the *Pax Mongolica*. As it turned out, Marco Polo's was an isolated instance of merchant adventuring of no immediate cultural potency. But thanks to Rustichello of Pisa, his *Travels* continued to dangle the lure of the East before the European imagination and would thus eventually contribute decisively to European expansion.

Meanwhile, to a degree often forgotten, the initiative in global travel turned to the Arabs, who ever since the dramatic rise of Islam in the century following Muhammad's death had already been widely wandering and surveying the earthly frontiers of their faith. A notable early instance is al-Mas'udi, a tenth-century historian and geographer whose extensive travels through the Muslim world from Spain to India and all places in between allowed him to make important empirical corrections to such Ptolemaic misconceptions as that of an enclosed Indian Ocean, for instance. Roughly a century later, the Persian polymath al-Biruni accompanied the Afghan sultan Mahmud of Ghazni on his invasion of the Punjab and with his *History of India* (1030) left the first Islamic portrait of the South Asian subcontinent, its land, cities, and peoples.

But the greatest of all medieval Muslim travelers—indeed, in the estimation of some the greatest traveler of any culture of any time—was the Moroccan pilgrim Abu 'Abdallah ibn Battúta, who set out for Mecca from his native Tangier in 1325 and did not return until he had logged more than 75,000 miles through much of Africa, Arabia, Central Asia, India, and China. He was really no more an explorer than Marco Polo, insofar as he generally followed the well-worn caravan routes of *Dar al-Islam*, the "Abode of Islam," and his interest in places was consistently secondary to his interest in people. But he did leave the first recorded description of a crossing of the Sahara desert—a notable feat of exploration in two respects, the crossing and the recording—and his multivolume *Rihla*, or "Journey," includes the only eyewitness reports on such peripheral and then little-known lands as Sudanic West Africa, the Swahili Coast, Asia Minor, and the Malabar coast of India for the better part of a century or more. It also includes some high adventure and shipwreck worthy of any great explorer. In sum, Ibn Battúta was perhaps the best medieval instance of the accidental explorer, the explorer in spite of himself.

Unless, of course, that distinction should really apply to Zheng He, the Muslim-born "Grand Eunuch" and court favorite of the Yongle emperor of China who undertook to lead seven formidable maritime expeditions through what he knew as the "Western Sea," the Indian Ocean, between 1405 and 1433. History has hardly known what to make of these voyages of the "treasure ships." They were certainly conceived on a massive scale in every dimension: the first voyage alone featured sixty-two strong oceangoing junks—each one of them perhaps ten times the size of anything afloat in Europe at the time—a fleet of 225 smaller support vessels, and 27,780 men. Each voyage lasted two years on average, and in sum they took in destinations from Indochina to East

4. An early-seventeenth-century Chinese woodblock thought to depict the enormous "treasure ships" of Zheng He, the commander of seven formidable maritime expeditions in the Indian Ocean between 1405 and 1433.

Africa and all coastal points in between. But they did not establish new ocean routes or find any unknown lands. These were political ventures, in the main. The admiral's purpose was to gather tribute, establish diplomatic relations, subdue potential enemies, lavish gifts on friends, and generally overawe the world on behalf of the emperor with a grand display of Chinese naval power.

Only with the sixth voyage to the east coast of Africa did Zheng He turn to something like original exploration, and although the seventh voyage of 1431–33 was the largest and most ambitious, insofar as it ultimately achieved more than 12,600 miles of ocean travel, its main significance to history is that it was emphatically the last. The death of the Yongle emperor in 1424 had already deprived Zheng He of his royal patron and restored the authority at court of a Confucian elite opposed to overseas adventuring. With the admiral's own death at sea in 1433, his supporters could not restrain the inward-turning tide. The great fleet was broken up, foreign travel forbidden, the very name of Zheng He expunged from the records in an effort to erase his example. In 1420 Chinese ships and sailors had no equal in the world, and the Indian Ocean was on the cusp of becoming a Chinese lake. Eighty years later, scarcely a deep-seaworthy ship survived in China, the Indian Ocean was closer to being an Arab lake, and improbable though it seemed, the cultural force behind global maritime exploration had moved decisively and irrevocably to Europe.

Chapter 4
The age of exploration

Having come this far and briefly surveyed the history of earthly exploration from the first dispersal of prehistoric man to the fifteenth-century "treasure ship" voyages of the Chinese, one might reasonably be skeptical of so quaint a notion as "the age of exploration." Exploration, as explorers themselves like to say, is a timeless aspect of the human condition: we are restless wanderers on this spinning orb; our nature is to wonder what is out there and to seek to see, understand, and possess it. Given that, given the long history of geographical discovery and human convergence before the Columbian moment of 1492, any attempt to single it out as heralding the age of exploration seems as arbitrary as it does Eurocentric. What about the eighth-century Arab penetration of the Indian Ocean? Or the tenth-century Norse penetration of the Atlantic? Or the thirteenth-century Mongol integration of Eurasia? Why does none of these earlier instances of territorial search and seizure ever warrant equal standing with the sixteenth-century Iberian one? Why do textbooks and teachers stubbornly privilege late-medieval and early-modern Europe when designating "the age of exploration"?

Because at the end of the day, having made full allowance for Greek, Roman, Arab, Norse, Polynesian, or Mongol achievement in terms of exploration and cultural reach, there remains something stubbornly unique and momentous about the late-medieval extrusion of European maritime power and the record of exploration associated with it. Or rather several things. First, it was global in reach. When Zheng He died at sea in 1433, vast stretches of the world remained even to him—the greatest sailor-explorer of his age—not just unknown and inaccessible but unimagined and unimaginable. Ninety years later, a Portuguese ship commanded by Ferdinand Magellan had circumnavigated the earth and thus taken the full and honest measure of it. After Magellan, men and women were living, for better or for worse, in one interconnected world. Africa, Asia, the Americas, and Europe had fallen into place on the map and in the mind, along with the seas that had once divided but now could be felt to unite them.

Second, it was unprecedented in scope and daring. Earlier explorations and cultural extrusions—with the isolated exception of the Polynesian—had proceeded piecemeal over contiguous lands or narrow seas. Explorers felt their way from valley to valley or from harbor to harbor, never venturing more than a few days' distance from the places they knew and generally sure of where they were going. Columbus more than anyone before him broke this tentative pattern. He knew that sailing west would bring him eventually to Asia: otherwise, he had little precise idea where he was going when he set off into the empty expanse of the mid-Atlantic. He thus initiated the world's first instance of a fully transoceanic cultural diffusion. Arab traders had long since made their cultural presence known on the Malabar coast of India, but they did so largely by coasting the familiar shores of the Indian Ocean. There had been much of this sort of thing. But the extrusion of an entire culture across the open expanse of an ocean like the Atlantic was notably different and wholly unprecedented when it began.

Third, it took. The exploration of the world by fifteenth- and sixteenth-century European mariners permanently and decisively altered the lineaments of global power and set human history on the broad common course that it still to this day follows. Consider, by way of illuminating contrast, the Polynesian exception to the usual pattern of coastal exploration. Unlike those Arab or Chinese shore-huggers who felt their way cautiously around the contiguous rim of the Indian Ocean, the Polynesians audaciously carried their culture in its simple entirety across vast expanses of open sea. They indisputably achieved a transoceanic cultural diffusion. But this never extended beyond the far-flung islands of the South Pacific and Madagascar, and once achieved, it developed in long-standing isolation from the rest of the world. The transoceanic diffusion that Columbus set in train respected no global limit and continued unrelentingly until it had made the world over in its image. Few single dates in past experience warrant the claims to significance made for them. But when Columbus and his men walked onto the island that they called San Salvador on October 12, 1492, they truly changed the course of global history: they set in motion a chain of events that continues to give political, economic, social, and even philosophical shape to the modern world today.

The epochal significance of the Columbian landfall should not, however, lead us to overstate the significance of Christopher Columbus himself to the history of exploration. This once-celebrated and now much-denigrated "Admiral of the Ocean Sea" may have been more persistent than most explorer-adventurers of his age; he may have been unusually adroit when it came to the all-important art of securing royal patronage. But he was far from being either the lone visionary or the arch villain of competing classroom mythologies. For one thing, his notion that one could reach the east by sailing west was perfectly conventional and generally accepted by the time he set sail from Palos on August 3, 1492, and if he had not inadvertently stumbled on the Americas two months later, someone else soon would have, and indeed did. In his confused cruelties too, in his inability to recognize the prior claims of the Caribbean peoples he encountered, Columbus was altogether a man of his time. As a Genoese merchant-navigator born on the cusp of the medieval and modern ages, he perfectly embodied the peculiar mix of faith, cupidity, ambition, and curiosity that took European explorers overseas and encouraged them to seize and subdue what they found. And though his accidental achievement may ultimately have eclipsed most others in terms of long-term significance, it was not an isolated one. It emerged from the crowded context of the Portuguese origins of high Atlantic exploration.

A passage to India

To look at the map, it may seem unsurprising that Portugal, a kingdom occupying the narrow seaboard fringe of the Iberian peninsula, should have played so prominent a part in the maritime turn of late-medieval Europe. In a strict geographical sense it was: no other place in Europe projects so obviously outward into the sea. Yet Portugal had little in the way of a maritime tradition before the fifteenth century. Nor had it much in the way of such essential maritime resources as timber, iron, and tar. As a seafaring culture, certainly, Portugal languished far behind the Mediterranean city-states of Venice and Genoa, and it was in fact the Vivaldi brothers of Genoa, Ugolino and Vadino, who evidently attempted the first westward passage to India in 1291, a full two centuries before their more famous compatriot. Traditionally, however, both Venice and Genoa oriented themselves eastward to the overland trade routes of Arabia, the Balkans, and the Levant. When the rise of hostile Ottoman power in these regions forced a reorientation of European trade to the western Mediterranean over the course of the fourteenth century, they were less well placed to compete, and the tables of maritime advantage turned slowly to Portugal.

From the standpoint of the history of exploration, the date to mark out is August 24, 1415, when a Portuguese armada overwhelmed Ceuta, a Muslim fortress and trade emporium on the Moroccan side of the Strait of Gibraltar. Traditionally seen as an African extension of the *Reconquista*—the centuries-long Christian seizure of the Iberian peninsula from the hands of the Muslim infidel—Ceuta also marks the advent of the age of exploration, if only for the commanding presence there of the Infante Dom Henrique, familiar to us as "Henry the Navigator." According to biographical legend, it was the capture of Ceuta that first suggested to Henrique the storehouse of wealth that was Africa and so turned him from crusading prince into princely sponsor of the exploration of the African Atlantic. Refusing the cares and temptations of courtly life in Lisbon, he made his way to the "Sacred Promontory" of Sagres in the Portuguese Algarve and there established at his villa a sort of center for cartography, navigation, and shipbuilding. Though no navigator himself—the sobriquet is a nineteenth-century English invention—Henrique knew a good one when he saw one. And though his famous "School of Navigation" has long since been discredited as a romantic embellishment on something far less sophisticated, he was evidently a generous patron of those first Portuguese captains involved in the maritime forcing of the North African shore. If not the presiding genius, he was something like the godfather of Atlantic exploration, the most famous of the precursors and inspirers of the age of European reconnaissance.

In any case, Henrique's own achievements are less significant historically than what his prominent example suggests about the motives behind the Portuguese turn to the sea. In speaking of these, Henrique's self-appointed chronicler, Gomes Eannes de Zurara, emphasized curiosity in the form of a "desire to know" what lay beyond the Canary Islands, eagerness to establish new trade routes to sub-Saharan Africa, eagerness to convert pagans to Christianity and to seek alliance with lost Christian kings, and, above all else, an urge to live up to an astrological horoscope that bound him "to engage in great and noble conquests" and "to attempt the discovery of things which were hidden from other men." This last is especially revealing of a medieval turn of mind and the inescapably medieval context of the age of exploration.

Henrique's was still a world of signs and portents, of legendary kingdoms, of crusading zeal and the desire for fame, of destiny and divination.

True, in Zurara's mention of a "desire to know" we get just a whiff of the Renaissance spirit with which the textbooks traditionally associate Europe's outward turn. But Henrique had little interest in knowledge for disinterested knowledge's sake. He wanted to know where the Saracens were, how strong, and how many. He wanted to find Prester John, the wise and godly patriarch who according to popular medieval legend ruled over a wealthy Christian realm somewhere in the unknown heart of Africa. He wanted to find the source of the gold he had seen in Ceuta, not so as to enrich himself—Henrique was in fact something of a pious ascetic—but rather to maintain his rabble of "knights and squires" in the lordly manner to which they were accustomed. And finally he wanted to do great deeds that would redound to his everlasting fame. In all of this we rightly sense the standard formula of Christian knight-errantry. The crusades were over, but Henrique's was still a chivalry-steeped world, and in exploration as he conceived it, the spirit of the crusades lived on. Exploration Iberian style was chivalric adventuring by other means.

As for Henrique's actual earthly objectives, they centered at first on the Canary Islands, a volcanic archipelago just off the northwest coast of mainland Africa that was later to prove the essential springboard to the Americas. It was only when his efforts to secure the Canaries for Portugal failed in the face of both Castilian and native resistance that Henrique and his captains turned to the cape-by-cape exploration of the northwest African coast. The most storied achievement today is Gil Eannes's 1434 doubling of Cape Bojador, a barely discernible protuberance of the Western Sahara at 27° north, and this did involve an innovative bit of current sailing. But it was otherwise as little noted at the time as the cape itself. Far more significant in the overall scheme of things was Nuno Tristão's landing in 1442 on Arguin, the small island off the western coast of today's Mauritania where two years later Henrique was to establish the first European slave-trading station in Africa. Dinis Dias rounded Cape Verde, the westernmost bulge of the African continent in 1445, and from there the die was cast. By the time of Henrique's death in 1460, the riches of the Guinea Coast—gold, ivory, pepper, and slaves—were within Portugal's grasp, and exploration had yielded to full-throated exploitation.

Any hope of easy eastward passage to India suffered a decisive check in 1474, when Lopo Gonçalves and Rui de Sequeira discovered the southerly trend of the African coast beyond the Bight of Biafra and today's Republic of Cameroon. For the next seven years, the Portuguese crown focused on fortifying its trading stations on the Guinea Coast against both hostile natives and Castilian interlopers. With the accession of the Infante Dom João in 1481, however, Portugal had a king no less committed to exploration than his great-uncle Dom Henrique had been. Taking the title of "Lord of Guinea" in order to emphasize his African claims, João redoubled Portugal's missionary and baptismal efforts on land even as he brought the full resources of the Guinea trades to bear on extending the reach of Portuguese ships at sea. Henrique's explorers had relied for the most part on small, two-masted, lateen-rigged caravels adapted from the ordinary coastal fishing and carrying trades. Under João the Crown sponsored the development of a three-masted, square-rigged carrack dedicated to long-range, high-seas voyaging.

In 1484, recognizing the difficulty of navigating without reference to the immovable Pole Star (which vanishes beneath the northern horizon south of the equator), João established a commission of astronomer-mathematicians to work out a reliable method for fixing latitude by observation of the solar meridian. He encouraged the refinement of such existing navigational instruments as the compass, astrolabe, and quadrant. And like Henrique before him, he sponsored the systematic study of the wind and current patterns on which successful exploration ultimately depended. Here, the great breakthrough was the *volta do mar*, literally the "turn of the sea," a navigational technique by which Portuguese mariners returned from Africa by sailing counterintuitively deep into the mid-Atlantic until in the vicinity of the Azores they picked up the dependable westerlies that would bring them safely home. In the history of Atlantic exploration, nothing is more significant than this—the fifteenth-century Portuguese discovery of the North Atlantic Gyre. Without his subsequent understanding of it, Columbus's westward venture to the Indies would have been inconceivable.

The climax of the Portuguese prelude to the age of exploration came on February 3, 1488, when two caravels and a square-rigged supply ship under the command of Bartolomeu Dias dropped anchor in Mossel Bay, about 230 miles east of what is now Cape Town. King João had dispatched this knight-errant of the royal household six months earlier, doubly charged with finding the legendary priest-king Prester John and an ocean passage to India. Prester John not surprisingly eluded him, and so very nearly did the passage, as Dias beat his way south against continual storm and adverse northerly currents. Finally, unable to do much else, Dias stood out to sea and sailed south-southwest for many days until around 40° south he providentially picked up the prevailing South Atlantic westerlies that carried him eastward around the southern tip of Africa without his even noticing it. Ptolemy was wrong after all. The Indian Ocean was not an enclosed sea (although it still needed the simultaneous overland explorations of Pêro da Covilhã and Afonso de Paiva to put this beyond doubt); it was accessible from the Atlantic by way of what Dias fittingly called the Cape of Storms and King João named the Cape of Good Hope.

It remained only for Vasco da Gama to force the passage that Dias had opened. Why he waited ten years to do so, or rather why the Portuguese crown delayed ten years before sending him out to do so, is an enduring question. Succession disputes and factional squabbles at court; the unsettling if inconclusive news of Columbus's landfall in the west; the length and difficulty of the cape route itself; the vast uncertainty of what lay beyond the cape: all of these discouraged any thought of an immediate return to the southern ocean. And when return finally came in 1497, it did so less in the form of a voyage of discovery than of an armed embassy. Setting off from Lisbon in four square-rigged carracks, da Gama made first for the Cape Verde Islands, a newly settled volcanic archipelago some 350 miles off the westernmost point of Africa. In a boldly original move, he then reached far out to the southwest well past the promontory of Brazil before bearing southeast for Dias's westerlies and the Cape of Good Hope. By the time he and his men moored at St. Helena Bay, a hundred miles north of the cape, they had been at sea for ninety-six days and so completed the longest ocean passage of any European explorers to that time. They then coasted the cape northward past a land they named Natal (after the Christmas nativity) until they reached the Muslim port of Malindi, where da Gama had the good sense to hire a local pilot to guide him across the Indian Ocean. The fond tradition that identifies this pilot with Ahmad ibn Majid, the most celebrated Arab navigator of his day, is just that: a fond tradition. But it takes nothing away from the achievement of da Gama's pilot to say that we do not know who he was. Not only did he come to the rescue of an expedition that was very likely all at sea, as it were, thus setting the pattern of European dependence on native guidance in these waters. He also, in effect, reintroduced India to a western people who had not been there since the days of Alexander the Great.

And thereby hung a long colonial tale. In the short term, the voyage of Vasco da Gama was a cocked-up affair that did little to displace either the existing overland trade routes to India or the traditional dispensation of power in the Indian Ocean basin. But the great Scottish economist Adam Smith, author of *The Wealth of Nations* (1776), ultimately ranked it alongside the Columbian discovery of America as one of the "greatest and most important events recorded in the history of mankind," one that eventually united "the most distant parts of the world" and made possible, for good and ill, the mercantile wealth of European nations.

Christopher Columbus and the "Enterprise of the Indies"

Among the many dubious legends surrounding the life of Christopher Columbus, that most mythologized of all of history's explorers, is one that places him in the welcoming crowd when Bartholomeu Dias and his three storm-tossed ships returned in triumph from the Cape of Good Hope to Lisbon in December 1488. It was Dias's success, the story goes, that killed any lingering interest the Portuguese Crown might have had in westward voyaging and so sent a disheartened Columbus back to Seville, where after a few more years of pleading and persuading he secured the backing of Ferdinand and Isabella of Spain.

Backing for what was never clear. More legend attributes to Columbus a long-held design of sailing west to China, and in his pitch to his royal patrons he had specifically emphasized this. But the terms of his commission signed at Santa Fe against the momentous backdrop of the conquest of Granada alluded vaguely to "islands and mainlands in the Ocean Sea," and for years Columbus had wavered indecisively among several alternative objectives, some real (Japan, China, India), some imagined (Antilia, the Seven Cities, the Antipodes). What remained consistent throughout was his plan to sail west. Beyond that he seemed less concerned about what he would discover than determined to discover something. And to discover it soon, for again contrary to romantic legend, Columbus was hardly alone or even unusual in his westward yearnings. Both in his adventurous form of social ambition and in his spherical form of geographical speculation, he was very much a man of his time. What he wanted most of all was to "discover something" in the western ocean before someone else like him did.

That said, no one else of Columbus's time brought precisely his set of experiences to bear on the challenge of oceanic discovery, and of these arguably the most important was his Genoese origin. Though not quite the place it had been before the rise of Ottoman power undermined its strategic position in the eastern Mediterranean, the Genoa of Columbus's youth was still one of the largest centers of maritime commerce in the world, a place where seafaring was a way of life and an obvious form of upward mobility for one of such humble birth as Columbus, the son of a weaver and tavern keeper. Positioned as it was on the Ligurian coast of the Italian peninsula, Genoa felt the call of the West more powerfully than Venice, its Adriatic counterpart, and served as a kind of maritime fulcrum in the slow turning of the center of European gravity from the Mediterranean to the Atlantic. Like all the city states it also nurtured the humanist spirit of the Renaissance. But biographers have overplayed Renaissance responsibility for Columbus. True, he was born just a year before da Vinci and partook of many of the intellectual advances of his age, especially where navigation and cartography were concerned. But his mind-set was stubbornly medieval, as was the dynastic lilt of his aspirations. Like Henrique's captains before him, Columbus thought of maritime exploration as a ship-borne form of Christian knight-errantry, and his life's overriding ambition was to escape the shame of his humble origin and found a noble dynasty of his own through oceanic feats of derring-do.

By the time he offered his "enterprise of the Indies" to King João of Portugal in 1484, Columbus was a seasoned navigator with extensive experience of Mediterranean and near-Atlantic waters. He was also a passable geographer, one whose quest for westward glory rested on a wide reading of ancient and modern authorities. Just when he read what is insufficiently clear, however, to settle the enduring question of whether he ever had a consistent notion of what he was up to. On balance the evidence suggests he did not: exploration for him was a means to rank and dignity more than a calling for its own sake, and his theoretical reasoning shifted along with his objectives to suit whatever audience of prospective patrons he found himself addressing.

Even so, through all the bluster and salesmanship, a few traceable themes emerge. From Ptolemy, for instance, or rather from that version of Ptolemy's *Geographia* that was enjoying a Renaissance revival in the fifteenth century, Columbus took his image of an elongated Eurasian landmass broken by one intervening "Ocean Sea." From Marco Polo he took both his visions of Asian splendor and his hopeful notion that Asia extended farther eastward into the Ocean Sea than even Ptolemy had thought. Eratosthenes's ancient estimate of the total circumference of the Earth was discouragingly large—250,000 stadia or (by the Egyptian standard of conversion), some 21,000 nautical miles. But such modern authorities as the French theologian-astrologer Pierre d'Ailly helped Columbus whittle this down in his mind to a less intimidating 16,000 and, more importantly, assured him that the Ocean Sea was likely so narrow as to be traversable in just a few days. The letters in which the Florentine humanist Paolo dal Pozzo Toscanelli allegedly encouraged Columbus in a westward venture to Asia are of uncertain authenticity. But Columbus was probably acquainted with Martin Behaim, the German cosmographer whose innovative globe of 1492—the oldest known and the last to represent the world as imagined before Columbus—places Japan more or less where Cuba should be and thus within striking distance of the Canaries.

In short, the combined influence of Ptolemy's flawed cartography, Marco Polo's *Travels*, the legends of antiquity, and a few tantalizing sailors' reports increasingly lured Columbus westward, and so secure at last in his longed-for title and dignity—Ferdinand and Isabella had promised to name him "Admiral of the Ocean Sea" and Viceroy and Governor of any lands he might discover—he weighed anchor on August 3, 1492, resolved, as he said in his journal, "to write down the whole of this voyage in detail, day by day, everything that I should do and see and undergo."

Of all of Columbus's decisions, this seemingly modest one to keep a journal was in some respects the most significant. By recounting his voyage in writing—something uncommon at the time—he ensured himself a place in history that no amount of disparagement has diminished. "The written record has become the touchstone of his achievement," as one of his many translators has said. More particularly, Columbus's journal made him the archetypal modern explorer, one who not only "found the new" but wrote about it, publicized it, spread the news of it abroad in such a way as to alter people's perceptions of the world they inhabited. He explored *and* discovered because he *disclosed*. More than anything else, it was this workaday journal that effected the "discovery" of "the New World" and that even in the redacted form in which it comes down to us continues to enact the confused thrill of that discovery in the minds of those who read it. After Columbus, exploration and writing become inextricable. There is no exploration, after 1492, without the exploration account.

As a navigator, Columbus's shrewdest stroke—and one made possible only by his Spanish sponsorship—was to make first for the Canary Islands off the northwest coast of Africa. Earlier forays into the Atlantic had set out from the Azores and come to grief in the face of prevailing westerlies. From the Canaries, Columbus picked up the northeast trades that swept his little flotilla directly across the Atlantic in a matter of thirty-three days. This was longer than he had been expecting, but if his speculations were otherwise accurate, then the little island first sighted from the *Pinta* on October 12 should have been an outlier of Japan. Instead it was one of the innumerable small islands of the Bahamas, probably. Columbus was off by about 8,000 miles as the very determined crow flies. Thus his painfully evident confusion over the course of the succeeding days as he struggles to reconcile the land and people before him with his hard-won illusions. In all the history of exploration, there is nothing like it, nothing like this first confused encounter of Spaniard and Taino Indian. Virtually all earlier encounters between Europeans and others had taken place across somewhat porous boundaries and had therefore been at least vaguely anticipated. Exploration had proceeded by fits and starts, by innumerable small acts of reconnaissance that prepared the exploring mind for what it might find. Columbus and his men, on the other hand, experienced the shock of extreme incommensurability. They found the new and unexpected to a degree unmatched before or since and with a force that left them literally unable to assimilate or comprehend it. They could, however, nevertheless take possession of it, which Columbus proceeded to do with all due ceremony, as if there were agreed formalities involved.

5. Theodor de Bry's fanciful and idealized rendering, a century after the fact, of Christopher Columbus's epochal landfall in the Caribbean. Originally captioned "Columbus, as he first arrives in India, is received by the inhabitants and honored with the bestowing of many gifts," it was one in a multivolume series of copperplate engravings that gave Europeans their first visual representations of North America.

His landfall thus secured and suitably renamed—another essential feature of the explorer's rite of taking possession—Columbus set about his Caribbean reconnaissance with two objectives in mind: to find his way to Japan and mainland China, and to find the source of the bits of gold he saw adorning the bodies of the natives. In both of these he was to be frustrated, and over the next few weeks as his cartographic confusion deepened, he began desperately to project his desires onto whatever it was that he had in fact found. When Cuba refused to resolve itself into Japan, it became perfect and marvelous in its own right, the sweetest and fairest land imaginable, the nearest thing to paradise on earth. The natives were all generosity and goodness, primitive to be sure but fully human, and in their sylvan innocence ready to accept the one true word of God. By the same token, they seemed easily overawed and subdued, and might make for slaves as readily as Christians if the search for gold truly failed and the need arose for some other exploitable resource. God and gold then, in one form or another, but overriding both of these familiar explorer's motives in Columbus's mind was that of his own glory. As landfall succeeded landfall and one misfortune after another beset his flotilla, the admiral somehow became more convinced of his divine anointment and began to imagine that the profits of his enterprise might ultimately pay for a Spanish reconquest of Jerusalem. Never mind China. By the time he turned for home in fevered bewilderment, Columbus was thinking of the ultimate Crusade: from Hispaniola to the Holy Land.

Ferdinand and Isabella, meanwhile, were sufficiently encouraged by Columbus's glowing reports to invest in a much larger voyage of colonization and settlement in 1493. It was this second voyage, complete with its cargo of horses, pigs, goats, sugarcane, oranges, and lemons, that would initiate what Alfred Crosby termed "the Columbian Exchange": the transoceanic transfer of plants, animals, peoples, and microbes that ended the environmental isolation of the American hemisphere and made, over time and at great human cost, for one conjoined, circum-Atlantic world.

Its history was grisly at the outset as all of Columbus's early illusions about native pliability proved as misplaced as his confidence in his own ability to restrain his compatriots' ruthlessness. As massacre succeeded massacre, Columbus sought refuge in further explorations, hoping to prove that Cuba, as it evidently was not Japan, had to be the Malay Peninsula. Only on the third voyage in 1498 did he finally sense the "New World" truth, and then only briefly. Standing off the coast of what Amerigo Vespucci would soon name Venezuela and observing the huge freshwater discharge of the Orinoco into the sea, Columbus came to a momentous realization and on August 14, 1498, wrote in his journal: "I believe this is a very great continental land that until now has remained unknown." It was the greatest discovery in the history of European exploration, and it does not diminish it much to add that within a few days the seer had trumped the scientist in Columbus—the medieval had trumped the modern— and he had decided that the "other world" he had found was actually the Terrestrial Paradise. Between them, his Christian cosmography and his Ptolemaic geography would allow for no other conclusion, and so, leaving Eden undisturbed, in his fourth and final voyage Columbus reverted to the north in a desperate effort to round Malaysia into what he still imagined must be the Indian Ocean on the other side.

But of course it was not Malaysia. It was the continuous littoral shore of Central America. And what lay on the other side was not the Indian Ocean at all but the vast and empty immensity of the Pacific.

From explorers to conquistadors

After Columbus and da Gama, anything, it seemed, was worth a try, and discovery followed on discovery in such rapid succession that understanding could not keep pace. When John Cabot—a one-time partner in Columbus's Enterprise of the Indies now sailing in service to Henry VII of England—became the first

European since the Norse to reach North America in 1497, he too thought he was in China, as did his first successors, the brothers Gaspar and Miguel Corte-Real, who rediscovered Greenland and the Labrador coast for Portugal before perishing at sea in 1502. Reaching the mouth of what may have been the Amazon in 1499, Vicente Yáñez Pinzón (erstwhile captain of Columbus's Niña) thought he had found the Ganges, and even Amerigo Vespucci, whom history generally credits with recognizing the true nature of the landmasses that bear his name, thought he was skirting a promontory of Asia when he rounded Brazil as far south as the harbor he called Rio de Janeiro in 1502. Only later, as loggers and explorers followed the Brazilian coast farther and farther south and the first conquistadors probed deeper and deeper into the Central American interior did the "New World" realization finally sink in. The German cartographer Martin Waldseemüller's suggestion that it be called "America" gave Vespucci more credit than he was due, and it took a long time to take hold. But by the time Vasco Núñez de Balboa crossed the isthmus of Panama under native guidance in 1513, thus becoming the first European to gaze westward over the "South Sea," the general picture was discouragingly clear: between Europe and the riches of the Orient lay a huge intervening landmass and at least one unexpectedly large ocean.

Soon the American landmass would come to be appreciated for its own sake and exploration would align itself with conquest; the explorer would turn *conquistador*. For the moment, however, judging from the Spanish experience in the Caribbean, the "New World" seemed altogether more trouble than it was worth, and the rival courts of Europe focused their energies on finding a way either through or around it. Thus appeared on the scene a new sort of specialist, the professional explorer, the maritime equivalent of those mercenary soldiers who at the same moment were making a profession of fighting for hire in Europe. Most were either Italian or Portuguese, but they wore their national identities lightly—unlike the explorers of a later age of empire—and sailed promiscuously for whomever stood most to benefit from, and pay for, their discoveries. Vespucci himself, a Florentine-born agent of the House of Medici turned master navigator of the House of Commerce at Seville, essentially defines the type. But none surpasses in either fame or achievement the all-purpose sailor of fortune known to his countrymen as Fernão de Magalhães and to history as Ferdinand Magellan.

Born into the Portuguese nobility around 1480, Magellan at a young age served as page to the queen consort, and his life never lost this courtly and chivalric luster. He was a gentleman adventurer, a knight errant who long before he set out on his circumnavigation had become addicted to daring deeds by land and sea. A veteran of many of Portugal's battles for maritime supremacy in the East—he was with Alfonso de Albuquerque at the climactic capture of Malacca in 1511—he also fought in North Africa before falling into disgrace for trade with the enemy. Reading reports of Vespucci's voyages and having spoken to the few surviving witnesses of Juan Díaz de Solís's discovery of the Río de la Plata in 1516, he became convinced that a passage to the East might yet be found through South America. But after da Gama's proof of the feasibility of the cape route, his own countrymen had no interest in such westward will-o'-the-wisps, and so in October 1517 Magellan easily transferred his allegiance and offered his project to Spain. Not quite two years later, on September 20, 1519, he sailed from Salúncar de Barrameda with a fleet of five small ships and a crew of 270 men.

What followed was the arguably the greatest epic adventure in the annals of exploration. After wintering in Patagonia and ruthlessly suppressing the first of several mutinies, Magellan found the strait that bears his name at 52° south—much farther south than he would have liked and a nasty piece of business too: shoal riven and storm tossed, a tortuous maze of shifting channels and swirling currents. By the time he emerged into what he called *Mar Pacifico* after the relative stillness of its waters, he had already lost two

6. The knight errant as explorer: a nineteenth-century facsimile engraving of Ferdinand Magellan, drafting compass and globe in hand, whose one surviving ship, *Victoria*, completed the first known circumnavigation of the earth in 1522 under the command of Juan Sebastián Elcano.

ships, exhausted his provisions, and essentially failed in his expeditionary purpose. Honor still beckoned though, and once having found favorable winds to the north, he set his course west for what he thought would be smooth sailing across a narrow, island-strewn sea.

It turned out to be a wide and largely empty sea, and by the time he finally found anchorage at Guam in the Marianas, Magellan and his crew had been reduced to eating rats and leather. Worse followed when in the Philippines Magellan's lust for adventure overcame his reason, and he died indulging a bit of mercenary soldiering on behalf of a local ruler. Much diminished in every respect, the expedition limped on to the Spice Islands under the command of Juan Sebastián Elcano who, after much more misadventure, brought one ship and eighteen men safely home by way of the Indian Ocean and the Atlantic, thus completing at terrible cost the first known circumnavigation of the earth. It was a notable feat pulled off with undeniable style, but it solved nothing where practical access to the East was concerned. After the failure of one follow-up expedition in 1525, the Spanish abandoned the Strait of Magellan and resolved to make the most of what they had inadvertently found in the Americas.

Thus from the 1520s the age of professional explorer gave way to the age of the conquistador. The distinction is somewhat artificial: exploration was after all a necessary precursor to the conquest, colonization, and social exploitation of any part of the New World, and Coronado in particular probably deserves to be remembered more as an explorer than a conquistador. His traverse of New Mexico and vast stretches of the southern Great Plains in 1540–42 yielded far more in geographical knowledge than it did in either wealth or conqueror's renown. More than one historian has resorted to the term "conquistador-explorer" to describe those legions of Spanish adventurers who fanned out across Central and South America in the sixteenth century, and it is a reasonable hybrid. But contemporaries would not have used it. They would have called men like Coronado *adelantados*, from the medieval military title meaning "advance men" or, literally, "those who go before." The conquistador was thus the advance man of empire in the Spanish New World, but he was not in any formal sense a soldier or agent of his king. In almost every case, a conquistador was a licensed private invader, an armed entrepreneur who undertook the exploration and occupation of a given region at his own or his backers' expense. If he lived, he had a chance of being named governor of a province of New Spain. If not, well then, a martyr to the cause of civilization.

From the Caribbean crucible of "New World" empire, the Spanish *entrada* into the Americas followed two distinct routes of exploration and conquest: from Cuba on to the Mexican mainland (Cortés) and from Hispaniola to the Isthmus of Panama and thence southward to Peru (Pizarro). Later, two more routes tended north: from the Caribbean to the Florida peninsula, Georgia, and the Appalachian south (de Soto) and from Mexico northward into the American southwest (Coronado). These were all well-traveled and well-populated routes by the time the Spanish arrived, and in every case the conquistadors relied more than they cared to admit on indigenous guides to lead them where they were going.

Not that they ever had a precise sense of destination. Like Columbus before them, they were drawn into the unknown by hopes of fame and fortune, and they would take either wherever they could find it. Mexico and Peru seemed to prove that the game was worth the candle: here there really were gold-rich kingdoms to conquer. But often the conquistadors were chasing after figments of their romance-steeped imaginations: El Dorado, the Seven Cities of Cíbola, the Fountain of Youth, the Philosopher's Stone, or the "Straits of Anián," that fabled passage through the North American continent that somehow against all reasonable evidence would persist as a goal of explorers even into the eighteenth century.

For the age of exploration was not yet one of objective, scientific observation, and the effect of every geographical discovery, it seems, was to encourage belief in yet another piece of fabulous geographical lore. From the modern point of view, for instance, the great achievement of Giovanni da Verrazano's voyage of 1525 was its demonstration of the continuous nature of the North American coastline from the Carolinas to Newfoundland. What most impressed Verrazano himself, however (misled as he was by a sighting of open water behind the barrier islands of North Carolina), was the evident narrowness of the American continent and the enticing proximity of the South Sea. Jacques Cartier's deep penetrations of the Canadian interior (1534–36) and Francis Drake's proof of the far westward reach of California (1577–80) ought to have made such a narrow conception impossible to sustain. But European maps, abhorring a vacuum, continued to accommodate a vast "Sea of Verrazzano" in the American interior until the late eighteenth century—until, that is, the Age of the Enlightenment, when fact began to displace fancy as the starting point of geographical speculation, and explorers began to show things as they really were, rather than as how they desperately wanted them to be.

Chapter 5
Exploration and the Enlightenment

Charles-Marie de La Condamine would not have described himself as an explorer. He was a mathematician and astronomer, an esteemed member of the French Académie Royale des Sciences. But his fame rests on his prominent participation in what has since been recognized as the prototype, in many respects, of the modern exploring expedition. The impetus to it came from a heated debate among European savants over the shape of the earth. For years, cartographers had noticed that the distance between any two given degrees of latitude did not appear to be uniform and that the earth could not, therefore, be a perfect sphere, as the ancients had imagined. Rather, it had to be either a "prolate spheroid," that is, distended conically toward the poles, as René Descartes believed, or an "oblate spheroid," that is, distended at the equator and flattened at the poles, as Isaac Newton believed. The increasing weight of evidence lay with Newton, but the followers of Descartes refused to yield on what seemed to them a point of national honor. In 1735, in hopes of settling the matter, the Académie Royale dispatched a scientific expedition to Quito in the Spanish Viceroyalty of Peru to measure an arc of latitude across the equator and thus—together with a complementary effort in the Arctic led by Pierre-Louis Moreau de Maupertuis—establish finally the true "figure of the Earth."

Led by the astronomer and mathematician Louis Godin and including, in addition to La Condamine, a notable company of scientists, surveyors, and engineers, the Geodesic Mission to the Equator as it came to be called sailed from La Rochelle on May 16, 1735. By the time it arrived via the Isthmus of Panama at the Pacific port of Manta ten months later, it was already too beset by internal animosities to proceed as one: while Godin and the main body moved on over the western cordillera to Quito, La Condamine and his fellow mathematician Pierre Bouguer busied themselves on the coast with astronomical observations and village explorations. Accompanied by a single servant and slave, La Condamine then struck out on his own via dugout canoe up the Esmeraldas River into the heart of the rain forest, where he fell under the spell of nature and marveled at the sophisticated uses to which Amerindians put such tropical plants as curare, chichona, and rubber. By the time he had endured a perilous crossing of the mountains to rejoin his compatriots at Quito, his interests had widened beyond geodesy to include the natural and human history of the equatorial region in all its many dimensions. Without quite meaning to, he had established a pattern characteristic of the age, one in which science and the intricate relationships among all natural and human phenomena came to the fore of exploratory travel.

For the moment, however, the geodesic business at hand still beckoned, and once reassembled at Quito, the expedition undertook it in earnest. From a trigonometric baseline on the plain of Yaruquí, about twelve miles east of Quito, these *caballeros del punto fijo*, as bemused locals called them, these "gentlemen of the fixed point" slowly surveyed their way south through a high Andean valley to the town of Cuenca—a distance of about 220 miles or 3.5 degrees of measured latitude. It was laborious and painstaking work made all the more difficult by inadequate funding, incompetent leadership, official obstruction, and local animosity, but finally after eight years Godin had a result that confirmed the Newtonian hypothesis: the earth was an oblate spheroid. That fact established, La Condamine shook the dust of the expedition off his feet and teamed up with Pedro Vicente Maldonado, the Spanish-American governor of the Esmeraldas Province, for a three-thousand-mile descent of the Amazon by canoe and balsa raft.

For this daring feat alone, La Condamine returned to Paris a hero, a distinctly new kind of explorer-celebrity whose genius partook of science and adventure in seemingly equal measure. He had not led the Geodesic Mission, and he did not garner its official scholarly laurels, but over time, thanks to his indefatigable literary efforts, he became inseparable from it in the public mind. Thus, when the great Prussian scientist-explorer Alexander von Humboldt undertook his own cosmic voyage to South America at the end of the eighteenth century, he thought of himself as following in La Condamine's footsteps and took time to visit the "hallowed ground" of Yaruquí, where his predecessor's pyramidal monuments to the Geodesic Mission already lay in suitably romantic ruin. In Humboldt, Enlightenment exploration found its culminating figure; it found its harbinger in La Condamine, that "cartographic conquistador," one scholar has called him, whose deft joining of cosmopolitan science to exotic travel and literary celebrity marked the arrival of a new breed of explorer for a new age, for the "Second Great Age of Discovery."

To speak so readily of a "Second Great Age of Discovery" is perhaps too dramatic. It assumes an interlude between the first and second ages that the historical record will not bear out. True, the exploratory energies of the Spanish and the Portuguese faded in the sixteenth century, but those of the Dutch, the English, the French, and the Russians were only just gathering, and from one corner of the world to the next, the work of geographical discovery wore on. The Dutchman Willem Janszoon made the first recorded European landfall on Australia in 1606. A few decades later, his countryman Abel Tasman, looking for a navigable passage from the Indian Ocean to the Pacific—stumbled on what he thought was the long-sought continent of Terra Australis but was in fact New Zealand—a place hitherto unknown to any people other than the Maori themselves. The Dutch did not altogether neglect the Western Hemisphere: they twice commissioned the Englishman Henry Hudson to find the fabled Northwest Passage to Cathay. But when these efforts ended only in the discovery of the frigid bay that bears Hudson's name, the Dutch for the most part staked their future on the East. The Dutch West India Company, founded in 1621 to monopolize Dutch trade in the Atlantic, contributed little to new exploration there; a century after its founding it did however sponsor the famous foray of Jacob Roggeveen into the Pacific that led inadvertently to the discovery of Easter Island, the most remote inhabited island on the planet.

The French, meanwhile, though not altogether immune to the lure of the East, began to appreciate North America for its own rich sake and so undertook its interior exploration from the early seventeenth century, when Samuel de Champlain reconnoitered the extensive tributary watershed of the St. Lawrence and then followed the river proper as far as Lake Ontario. In 1634 Champlain's linguist, Jean Nicollet, carried on as far as Lake Michigan, where natives told him of a great river that swept toward the sea, but it would be almost another forty years before the fur trader Louis Jolliet and the Jesuit Father Jacques Marquette found the Mississippi, and still another ten before René-Robert de La Salle followed it to the Gulf of Mexico and claimed its entire watershed for King Louis IX of France. All of these explorations of interior North America depended on considerable native assistance. Everywhere the French went, they were guided by Hurons or Ottowas or Petúns or Miamis or various other Iroquoian or Algonquian peoples who had lived in the Great Lakes region for centuries and for whom it needed no discovering. Here, as usually elsewhere, exploration was less about original discovery than disclosure and cultural encounter on "the middle ground" between hitherto isolated peoples and empires.

As in North America, so in Siberia, animal furs were the main incentive to seventeenth-century exploration, although the Russian state was also quite eager to extend its tributary authority as far eastward as it could. In 1639, the Cossack Ivan Iur'ev Moskvitin crossed the remote but otherwise unimposing Dzhugdzhur Mountains east of the Lena Valley and followed the Ul'ia River to the Sea of Okhotsk, thus claiming the honor of the first Russian discovery of the Pacific. A few years later, Vasilii Danilovich Poiarkov brutally staked out what ultimately became the Sino-Russian frontier along the Amur River, and in 1648 Semen Ivanovich Dezhnev explored the Arctic extremities of eastern Siberia and made the first known passage of the strait that separates Asia from North America. The English, for now, could claim no such original achievement, though at the end of the century the irrepressible William Dampier made several roving voyages that elucidated some of the geographical mysteries of the East Indies. He was much more pirate-adventurer than explorer, but he nevertheless had a keen eye for local detail, and his writings, especially the enormously popular *New Voyage Around the World* (1697), did much to stimulate public interest in the Pacific and its aboriginal peoples.

Far from being an interlude then, the century or so following the Age of Exploration was one of unbroken activity and the relentless assertion of European expansionist energies. Even so, with the eighteenth-century Enlightenment comes a new exploratory logic that the Geodesic Mission to the Equator helps to elucidate. Never before had so large and learned a group of Europeans headed into the remote interior of the New World for an expressly scientific purpose. Never before had two European nations cooperated so explicitly in pursuit of a scientific goal. And never before had the results of an expedition been so elaborately publicized in maps, journals, and official reports back home. Columbus, for instance, had kept his maps and sailing directions to himself for fear of interlopers on what he regarded as his privileged commercial domain. For him, as for explorers of the late-medieval and early-modern periods generally, geographical understanding was a mere by-product of voyages aimed primarily at gold and glory; it was a means to the end of mercantile or military advantage, little valued for its own sake and never held up as the point or purpose of an exploratory venture. Gradually, however, as the scientific revolution encouraged ever-widening inquiry into the true nature of all things, exploration came to be regarded as an essential source of earthly knowledge. And by the time of the high Enlightenment it had become centrally concerned with the gathering of information about man and the natural world.

Not that the age-old concerns of commercial or strategic advantage ever fell away; there is nothing inherently benign or disinterested about scientific inquiry, and as a vast body of demystifying scholarship has shown, the Enlightenment was every bit as steeped in colonial assumptions as any other episode in European history. But those who see Enlightenment exploration as just another form of conquest, who see scientific travel as purely grasping and appropriative of the exotic, non-European "other," have overstated or at least oversimplified their case. It was not for nothing that explorers like La Condamine prided themselves on their humanity relative to those who had preceded them, and however much a figure like Humboldt might have exhibited the cultural arrogance of his age, he took an interest in the fate of indigenous peoples and was at least as active in resisting the course of European empire as he was in furthering it. Moreover, to dwell exclusively as many do on the "fatal impact" of eighteenth-century exploration on indigenous cultures is to disregard too easily the two-sidedness of the encounter and the capacity of some of those cultures to absorb, transform, ignore, or even resist the European incursion. It is to deny the possibility of the unexpected and the contingent nature of the explorer's knowledge. Exploration is never monolithic or straightforwardly hegemonic: it is fraught, ambivalent, confused, and paradoxical. And in the Enlightenment especially, it awkwardly combined hubris and humility, power and vulnerability, instrumental reason and a romantic willingness to be dwarfed as well as command.

The voyages of Captain Cook

In no single figure do the mixed motives and opposing tendencies of Enlightenment exploration come into such high relief as in Captain James Cook, the great English mariner who in the course of his three Pacific voyages between 1768 and 1779 "fixed the bounds of the habitable earth, as well as those of the navigable ocean," as an admiring contemporary said. If the Pacific Ocean was the Enlightenment's "New World," then Cook was its Columbus. He did not in any sense "discover" the Pacific; nor was he even the first eighteenth-century seaman to sojourn among its island peoples. But he was the first to take full measure of both, to bring order, coherence, and completion to the map of the Pacific from the Arctic to the Antarctic, and to disclose to the world the broad lineaments of Polynesian cultures. His personal ambition led him "not only farther than any man has been before me," as he put it, "but as far as I think it possible for man to go." For this he is the explorer's explorer. But although bold, Cook was not reckless. His voyages set an altogether new standard for maritime safety and well-being, and their significance goes far beyond the attainment of such arbitrary geographical objectives as his famous ne plus ultra of 71°10´ south. They contributed decisively to the development of such established disciplines as astronomy, oceanography, meteorology, and botany, and to the founding, in the next century, of such new ones as ethnology and anthropology. They also did much to integrate Oceania into modern systems of global trade even as they stimulated the Romantic imagination and its fondness for the primitive and the exotic.

No single individual, however extraordinary, can exert so broad an influence as all this: Cook's voyages were highly collaborative ventures involving patrons, artists, scientists, publishers, politicians, state officials, and military officers, all of whom shaped in different ways their purpose, course, and outcome. The impetus to the first voyage, for instance, came from the Royal Society of London, Great Britain's leading scientific academy, whose members were eager to obtain an accurate observation of the impending Transit of Venus across the sun. To this quintessentially scientific objective—one on which the calculation of the distance between the earth and the sun depended—the Admiralty then quietly added several commercial and strategic ones. Having observed the transit from the perfectly placed and recently discovered island of Tahiti, Cook was to resume the age-old search for Terra Australis Incognita, the great "unknown southern land" that had teased the European geographical imagination since the days of Vespucci, and assess its potential for exploitation and settlement. Failing that, he was to make a thorough survey of New Zealand, exploring as much of its unknown coasts as the condition of his ship and health of his crew would allow, and also take possession in the name of his king of any hitherto undiscovered islands that he might happen to encounter in the course of his voyage.

Thus instructed, Cook sailed from Plymouth aboard His Majesty's Bark *Endeavour*—a refitted collier of a sort with which he would have been familiar from his North Sea days—on August 26, 1768. Of the many supernumeraries on board, the most notable was Joseph Banks, already at age twenty-five a Fellow of the Royal Society and prominent gentleman naturalist. Though not responsible for the observation of the Transit of Venus—this work fell to Cook himself and the astronomer Charles Green—Banks presided over his own ambitious scientific program in that all-embracing manner characteristic of the eighteenth century— which is to say that he caught and studied and collected and classified everything that fell under his wondering gaze, whether animal, vegetable, or mineral. His retinue of eight included the botanist Daniel Carl Solander, a student of the great Swedish naturalist Carl Linnaeus, and two artists, Sydney Parkinson and Alexander Buchan, neither of whom survived the voyage but whose drawings and sketches amounted to the first comprehensive visual representations of the South Seas.

Initially bemused by all the scientific fuss, Cook was eventually impressed and over the course of the voyage not only befriended Banks but became something of a natural historian himself. Outside of navigation and cartography, Cook was not a particularly educated man, but his cabin on the *Endeavour* nevertheless became one of the courts of natural philosophy. With Cook, the Enlightenment had put out to sea.

By way of Rio and Cape Horn, Cook reached Tahiti seven weeks before the Transit of Venus on April 13, 1769. He had been preceded there by Samuel Wallis and the HMS *Dolphin* in 1767 and by the Frenchman Louis-Antoine de Bougainville, whose circumnavigation of 1766–69 set a limited precedent for Cook's in respect of scientific travel. But neither Wallis nor Bougainville had stayed very long, and it was Cook and company who fixed Tahiti in the European imagination and turned it into a trope of tropical paradise.

The real Tahiti was not paradise, of course, but a place already rife with European diseases and embroiled in internal wars and dynastic struggles. Thievery (at least from the European point of view) was endemic, and within two days one of Cook's officers had shot a man dead for seizing a musket. This was brutal retaliation, and it strained relations at the outset. But in time, mutual curiosity overcame mutual suspicion and made for the first sustained and reasonably peaceable encounter between European and Polynesian peoples. Cook's main concern remained the transit. But from the first days of his Tahitian sojourn, his journal exhibits a growing curiosity about local custom and a proto-anthropological way of thinking. It was a new stance on the part of the European explorer and one that allowed for true, if confused, interaction and at least some level of mutual understanding and regard.

Both were certainly apparent, the interaction and the mutual regard, when Tupaia, a high priest and all-around island dignitary, adviser and lover to the queenly chieftain Purea, presented himself aboard *Endeavour* and declared his intention to accompany her to England. Cook initially demurred, not wanting to come away with anyone to whom he could not promise return. But Banks was eager to add so dignified a curiosity to his collection and prevailed on the captain to give his consent, for which Cook soon had reason to be grateful, for Tupaia turned out to be both an estimable philosopher in his own right and a first-class mariner with extensive knowledge of Polynesian waters. Sometime after leaving Tahiti he painstakingly drew for Cook a chart of the South Pacific centered on his home island of Ra'iatea and showing the relative positions of seventy-four others. From then until his death of dysentery in Batavia (now Jakarta), Tupaia served not only as Cook's pilot but also as his roving ambassador, his cultural mediator with every community *Endeavour* encountered from the Society Islands to New Zealand and beyond. Deeply learned, he also schooled both Cook and Banks in Polynesian language, custom, and ritual, thus making his own essential contribution to early Pacific anthropology.

All this was altogether new. Since the days of Columbus explorers had relied on impressed native guides. But Tupaia was a willing partner in an enterprise that he came to regard as in some sense his own. His presence on board the *Endeavour* essentially altered the political dynamics of the voyage and lent it a cross-cultural bearing that no previous voyage of exploration had ever had.

Having completed the first known circuit of the islands of New Zealand and thus proven decisively they were not part of a great antipodal continent, Cook sailed west and made the first European landfall on the east coast of Australia on April 19, 1770. From the broad estuary that he named Botany Bay (after the many plant specimens Banks collected there), he crept his way painstakingly north through the labyrinth of the Great Barrier

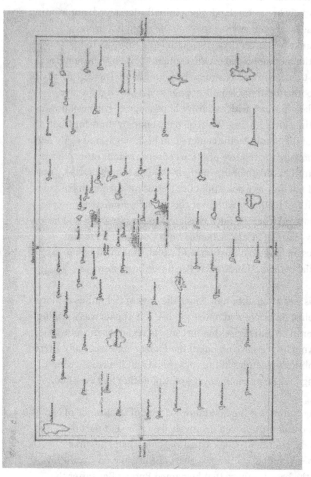

7. Tupaia's chart of the Pacific islands was drawn for Captain James Cook aboard *Endeavour* in 1770. Found among the papers of Joseph Banks, the chart mixes European and Polynesian geographies, and proves the collaborative, cross-cultural nature of Pacific exploration.

Reef as far as the Torres Strait and thence home, via the Dutch port of Batavia and the Cape of Good Hope. In sum he had charted 5,000 miles of previously unknown coastline, placed New Zealand and Australia accurately on the world's map, made contact for good and ill with innumerable Pacific peoples, and kept his ship and crew remarkably free from the ravages of scurvy. He had successfully observed the Transit of Venus and collected an unprecedentedly rich body of material—journals, logbooks, charts, drawings, paintings, scientific specimens—that disclosed for the first time to the world at large the wonders of the South Pacific. He had left England a formidable seaman; he returned an explorer.

And still the first voyage was a mere prelude to the second, the great southern voyage of 1772–75 that still stands for some as the most notable in history. The object this time was to settle finally the question of Terra Australis and generally pursue discoveries in as high a southern latitude as possible. In Banks's place as naturalist came Johann Reinhold Forster and his brilliant son Georg, whose subsequent account of the voyage has endured as a classic of Enlightenment travel literature. William Hodges, a student of the English landscape painter Richard Wilson, came along as expedition artist and set an altogether new and high romantic standard in that capacity. But the most important newcomer was a clock, a faithful replica of John Harrison's famous marine chronometer that in Cook's able hands finally solved the long-standing riddle of how to establish longitude at sea.

In command of *Resolution* and accompanied this time by the sister ship *Adventure*, Cook and his men made the first known crossing of the Antarctic Circle in January 1773. Finding nothing but fog and ice they retreated to New Zealand, from where Cook then set out on a giant loop of exploration that took him north to Pitcairn Island, westward through the Society and Cook Islands to Tonga, and then south again to New Zealand. In December 1773 he crossed the Antarctic Circle again and probed the ice as far as

71°10´ south, where he sensed the nearness of a frozen land that he could not and never did see. From there he sailed north and undertook an even wider sweep of the Pacific that took in Easter Island, the Marquesas, Tahiti, Tonga, the New Hebrides, and New Caledonia. Most of these had been glimpsed before by earlier European voyagers: Cook did not in any sense discover them. His contribution was to bring order and coherence to the confusion of the earlier maps and reports, to replace vagueness and conjecture with a new precision and accuracy. That done, he was satisfied. "I flater my self that the intention of the Voyage has in every respect been fully Answered," he wrote in his journal, "the Southern Hemisphere sufficiently explored and a final end put to the searching after a Southern Continent, which has at times ingrossed the attention of some of the Maritime Powers for near two Centuries past and the Geographers of all ages."

Having disposed of one great earthly conundrum, it remained only for Cook to take up the other, and in July 1776, now a full Post-captain and Fellow of the Royal Society, he set out again with *Resolution* and *Discovery* to resume the age-old search for the Northwest Passage, that fabled sea-route from the Atlantic to the Pacific that had eluded explorers since the days of Frobisher and Hudson. Unlike his predecessors, however, Cook would try to find it from the west, that is, from the Pacific side of the American continent, somewhere between 45° and 65° north. He had been preceded in these waters by Vitus Bering, the Danish navigator who in the service of Peter the Great had explored the strait that bears his name in 1728. But Bering had made no attempt on the Northwest Passage, and the maps derived from his expedition were flawed in any case: here again, Cook's would be not the first but the definitive effort.

From the Cape of Good Hope Cook made east for New Zealand and then north for Tonga, where owing to the lateness of the season he lingered for eleven weeks and entered into sustained and increasingly complex relationships with the indigenous chiefs.

No longer just Cook or even "Toote," as the Tahitians called him, he was now the compound self that his biographers describe, the part-English, part-Polynesian navigator-chief who was about to succumb to the fatal temptation of native adulation. Of the three voyages it was the third, with John Webber along as artist, that inspired the fullest descriptions and illustrations of the Polynesian peoples, in part because of Cook's deepening identification with them. Yet he was also increasingly exasperated and prone to violent temper, and the name he gave to the Tongan group, "the Friendly Islands," was belied by simmering violence and a contemplated plot on his life. Cook was indeed the greatest sailor of his age, but now he was navigating cultural waters that he could not fully fathom and exploring worlds of custom and ritual where he could not safely dwell.

Cook fulfilled one ancillary goal of the third voyage in September 1777, when he returned Omai, a native Ra'iatean who had come to London with *Adventure* three years earlier, to Huahine in the Society Islands. Sailing north from Kiritimati in the Line Islands, he next stumbled unexpectedly on Hawai'i, the northerly limit of the Polynesian diaspora and one hitherto unknown to the west. This was a major "discovery" but leaving it largely unexplored for now, Cook sailed on for "New Albion" and followed its coastline northward from the vicinity of today's Oregon as far as Alaska, westward along the Alaskan Peninsula, and then north again into the Bering Strait and across the Arctic Circle. He probed and charted everywhere he could as far as 70°14′ north before concluding that the Northwest Passage was an icy bust. A midshipman aboard *Discovery*, one George Vancouver, would later return to these same waters to put the matter beyond all doubt, but for his part Cook was done. He retreated for the winter to Hawai'i where he outstayed his welcome and was killed in a scuffle with the natives on February 14, 1779.

The death of Captain Cook on the shores of Kealakekua Bay propelled his reputation far beyond mere fame into the exalted realm of martyrdom. Renowned in life, he was sanctified in death and held up as a paragon of Enlightenment virtue, a victim of his own humanity, and without question "the most moderate, humane, and gentle circumnavigator that ever went upon discoveries," as one admiring contemporary, the novelist Fanny Burney, put it. Posterity, needless to say, has been less kind, and in Polynesia especially Cook is reviled as the serpent in the garden, as the leading agent of a western intrusion that destroyed the delicate basis of independent island civilization. Cook himself inclined occasionally toward the latter view and regretted how he and his crew had introduced "wants and diseases" the islanders had never known before and disturbed "that happy tranquility they and their fore Fathers had injoy'd."

Not that such romantic regret ever stopped him from seeing the job through or taking possession in the name of his king. But Cook was no colonizer. For him, the act of taking possession was a rhetorical one that marked his progress as an explorer; his practice of conferring his own names on the islands was not proto-imperial but directional and navigational. And once having named and thus marked a place, Cook's preference was to leave it as he found it. However intrusive his presence, his interventions in Polynesian life were tentative and tactical, and partook of no civilizing mission. The many who followed him into the South Pacific were less restrained, and to that extent Cook may be held inadvertently accountable for aiding and abetting a colonial process he himself did not envision. Neither paragon nor villain, he was a consummate seaman whose mixed achievement was to have left the world a considerably less mysterious place than he found it.

Enter romanticism

"Geography is a science of facts," Louis Antoine de Bougainville had insisted in a widely read account of his circumnavigation of 1766–69, and Cook had for the most part clung to this rationalist precept as he methodically disposed of one geographical illusion after another. But Cook lingered far longer in the Pacific than his French predecessor had done and in the end proved more susceptible to its aesthetic allure. He was no romantic, but his journal exhibits an occasional tendency toward metaphysical rapture, as when, for instance, he digresses on the simultaneous beauty and horror of the Antarctic ice fields. William Hodges, artist on Cook's second voyage, drew criticism from his neoclassical contemporaries for his overly imaginative handling of atmospheric effects: his paintings are remarkable precisely for combining the descriptive and the impressionistic. And in Georg Forster, the young assistant naturalist on the second voyage, the attitude of aesthetic wonder comes fully alive. In all these respects, Cook's voyages anticipate the modern intersection of science, exploration, and romance. They anticipate, as it were, the coming of Humboldt.

Born in 1769, the year of the Transit of Venus, Alexander von Humboldt was a true child of the Enlightenment. His first tutor was the German translator of *Robinson Crusoe*, Daniel Defoe's classic salute to man's innate ingenuity. His early schooling featured immersions in mathematics, physics, and botany, and his interests ran so strongly toward collecting plants and herbal specimens that he became known in his family as "the Little Apothecary." Electricity, chemistry, and geology all absorbed him by turns but never to the exclusion of art, music, or poetry. A genuine polymath, Humboldt moved in sophisticated intellectual circles that included Goethe, Schiller, and other leading lions of German Romanticism. From Immanuel Kant he derived his sense of the limits to human reason and of the importance of aesthetic sensitivity and intuition in penetrating beyond surface phenomena to the inner realities of things. As an explorer, this was to prove his distinguishing characteristic. Not only did he have a wider range of scientific interests than any other explorer before him; he also combined his objective science with a subjective philosophy of wonder and thus saw unities and organic

77

relations where Joseph Banks, for instance, had seen discreet objects and isolated natural effects. Although he thought of himself more as a scientific traveler than explorer, Humboldt had enough "uncertain longing for the distant and unknown," as he once put it, to qualify emphatically as both. He was as adventurous as he was scholarly, and his hybrid example influenced the exploratory ideal right down to the twentieth century.

Humboldt's initiation into the art of scientific travel came in 1790, when he accompanied Georg Forster on a tour of the Low Countries. Forster had been with Cook, and through him Humboldt absorbed some of the great captain's legacy. More importantly, though, Forster taught Humboldt how to see and feel, how to combine close empirical observation with aesthetic judgments and emotional responses to land and landscape. For most of the succeeding decade, Humboldt dabbled in experimental science while working as an inspector for the Prussian Department of Mines. But his tour with Forster had sealed his determination one day to undertake a great journey of his own. When an opportunity to accompany a new French expedition to the South Pacific fell through, he made his way to Madrid, where his reputation as a geologist caught the attention of a Spanish Court eager to exploit the mineral resources of its American dominion. Humboldt's purposes were not exploitative, but he was not above currying favor as needed, and so armed with royal passports and the rare privilege of unlimited access to Spanish territories, he and his traveling companion, Aimé Bonpland, sailed for the new world on the mail boat *Pizarro* on June 5, 1799.

They meant to go to Cuba, but the outbreak of fever on the *Pizarro* forced a shorter Atlantic passage, and Humboldt found himself disembarking more or less precisely where Columbus had made his continental landfall in 1498. This was an apt coincidence, for after five years of arduous travel through some of the continent's hinterlands, Humboldt was to find himself widely celebrated as "the *second* Columbus," the second and indeed "the *true* discoverer of America," as Simón Bolívar said, for whereas Columbus had merely laid the land open to plunder and conquest, Humboldt saw it on its own terms and gave it a geographical identity separate from European ambition. Critics of Enlightenment science would demur and say that to scrutinize South America so closely was to appropriate it all the more fully to European control, and it is true that one cannot extricate Humboldt from the colonial context in which he moved. It is also true, however, that he was an outspoken critic of European colonialism who combined his Enlightenment-derived confidence in the power of reason with a romantic sense of human vulnerability. His science had heart and led him on occasion to surprisingly egalitarian and even ecological conclusions.

Guided by a Guayqueria Indian named Carlos del Pino, Humboldt and Bonpland spent the first six months of their odyssey exploring the coastal regions of New Andalusia. They then sailed west to Caracas, from where they crossed the coastal mountains and moved south across the arid steppes and grasslands of the Orinoco basin. For years, European armchair explorers had indulged the legend of the Casiquiare, a remote and marvelously reverse-flowing river that somehow against all geographical logic joined the two otherwise independent river systems of the Amazon and the Orinoco. Humboldt needed to see this marvel or else prove it false in the manner of Cook, and so, at the remote Capuchin mission of San Fernando de Apure, he and Bonpland loaded a large sailing canoe called a *lancha* with a month's provisions and crates of scientific instruments and headed up the Orinoco into the heart of the tropical rainforest.

They were not alone. With them came guides, interpreters, rowers, and an ever expanding menagerie of caged and free-roaming animals. When the rapids of the upper Orinoco proved too much for the *lancha*, smaller canoes took over and carried the party beyond the Great Cataracts into the great unknown.

Somewhere in the vicinity of mission San Fernando de Atabapo, they left the Orinoco and portaged overland to the Rio Negro, the large left tributary of the Amazon that carried them down to the fabled Casiquiare. Here even Humboldt very nearly lost heart as the expedition became less a wilderness romance than a grim struggle for survival against the forces of elemental nature. Famished and fevered, consumed by insects, assailed on all sides by crocodiles and jaguars and not a little lost, the band pressed on until, finally, after a journey of six months and 1,725 hard-won tropical miles—vindication: the Casiquiare returned them to the Orinoco three leagues above the Esmeralda mission. The legend was true; the two great river systems of the South American continent were paradoxically joined. With that established, Humboldt wanted to ascend the Orinoco to its ultimate source amid the peaks of the Sierra Parima. But the curare-tipped arrows of the indigenous Yanonami sufficed finally to discourage even his wandering ambition, and with Bonpland near dead of dysentery the party retreated downriver to Angostura, then the capital of Spanish Guiana.

The Casiquiare crossing was Humboldt's greatest exploratory achievement, but it was not the one that made him famous. After a recuperative sojourn in Havana, he and Bonpland returned to South America and followed the spine of the Andean Cordillera from Bogotá to Quito. This was impressive enough, especially in that it led to a revolutionary new understanding of volcanic forces, the discovery of the earth's magnetic equator, and breakthroughs in the study of alpine ecology, mineralogy, and climatology. But the single day that stood out was June 23, 1802, when he and Bonpland and their revolutionary young friend Carlos Montúfar, who had joined the expedition at Quito, attempted to climb Chimborazo, then thought (mistakenly) to be the highest peak in the Americas. A huge crevasse stopped them just short of the summit, but at 19,734 feet above sea level they had climbed higher than anyone else on record. Theirs was the literal high point of exploration in the Enlightenment.

8. The romantic naturalist as explorer: Ferdinand Keller's 1881
depiction of Alexander von Humboldt and Aimé Bonpland in camp
with their native retinue on the Orinoco in 1800.

But it was also the point at which Humboldt discovered the
limits of Enlightenment science and the insignificance of *Homo
explorans* in the cosmic scheme of things. Here in the blinding
snow and bitter cold of 19,000 feet, his precious instruments
availed him nothing, and his senses failed him too as, snow-blind

and bleeding, frost-bitten and injured, he reeled in a hypoxic stupor from one ice-encrusted rock to the next. Later, once safely down from the mountain, Humboldt set about putting a proper scientific face on the experience: his chart depicting the climate zones of Chimborazo is a frequently reproduced classic of nineteenth-century graphic representation. But he never quite forgot the pointless exhilaration he felt on having simply been where no human had been before, on having tested himself against an extreme environment and survived. High on Chimborazo, for a day at least, the scientific traveler yielded to the romantic adventurer, the instrumental yielded to the human, and a new epoch tentatively opened in the history of global exploration.

Chapter 6
Exploration and empire

"How I long to be in Paris," Humboldt wrote from Lima in November 1802, not long after his Andean traverse essentially completed his South American explorations. Far more than Prussia, the land of his birth, Paris, the unrivaled center of European science, tugged at his cosmopolitan heart, and it was there that he would eventually turn to writing up the voluminous results of his travels. For now, however, he could not resist the "moral obligation," as he put it, to see the United States—since the advent of Napoleon the world's only passable republic—and, if possible, meet Thomas Jefferson, the fledgling republic's resident philosopher-president. After lingering for a year in Mexico then, he made his way first to Philadelphia, where he was the honored guest of the American Philosophical Society, the country's oldest and most prestigious learned body, and then to Washington and the newly built White House, where he and Jefferson engaged in animated discussions of topics ranging from woolly mammoths to plant ecology, Indian languages, Mexican politics, and the untold mysteries of the North American interior. As it happened, just as the two men were meeting, Captains Meriwether Lewis and William Clark were leading Jefferson's famous "Corps of Discovery" up the Missouri River and into the heart of the Great Plains. Humboldt would have been eager to hear about this and must have regretted that he had arrived in the United States just too late to meet the explorers themselves and compare notes on the art of wilderness travel.

For the Lewis and Clark expedition, as history knows it, was in many respects cut from Humboldtian cloth. Jefferson too was a man of the Enlightenment, president not only of the United States but of the American Philosophical Society, and he had carefully instructed Lewis to attend to "the soil and face of the country," its flora and fauna, its climate and weather patterns, its fossils and "mineral productions," its "volcanic appearances" and, of course, its people: not just their tribal names and numbers, but their languages, traditions, monuments, their "ordinary occupations," their "moral & physical circumstances," their "laws, customs & dispositions." In short, Lewis and Clark's was to be a scientific and ethnographic expedition of the sort that would have done Humboldt proud. Theirs was a corps of varied and all-purpose discovery.

In other respects, however, Lewis and Clark mark an important departure from the Age of Humboldt where exploration is concerned. When Jefferson first conceived of their expedition, the vast territories through which it was to travel were still claimed by France and Spain, and a Scottish explorer named Alexander Mackenzie had completed an overland crossing of Canada and thus renewed a presumptive British claim to the Pacific Northwest. All of this worried Jefferson, whose vision of a sturdy republic of independent yeoman farmers rested on the possibility of infinite westward migration. France ceded the Louisiana Territory to the United States in 1803, thus lowering the geopolitical urgency somewhat, but the expedition that set out a year later was still above all an imperial reconnaissance, an exploratory expression of American expansionism. Its two overriding purposes were to find a practicable water route across the North American continent and to establish peaceful relations with the native peoples now manifestly destined to come under American rule. Each of these purposes Jefferson couched in appropriately commercial and humanitarian terms, but that he organized what was, after all, a small military mission to carry them out speaks to his essentially annexationist intentions. His scientific interests were genuine, but Lewis and Clark were his diplomats in buckskin: they were less philosopher-adventures à la Humboldt than soldier-explorers whose line of march would mark a putative border between the United States and British Canada.

The Lewis and Clark expedition completed the first overland crossing of the eventual United States and reached the Pacific Ocean at the mouth of the Columbia River on November 18, 1805. A day later and half a world away, a Scottish explorer named Mungo Park set off on what he hoped would be the first descent of the Niger River from its source in the Guinea Highlands to the sea. The Niger had beguiled the European imagination from ancient times, when Pliny the Elder guessed on the basis of its rumored eastward course that it somewhere flowed into the Nile. Like Jefferson's imagined Missouri, the Niger thus held out the promise of easy transcontinental passage, but it added to that the old allure of fabled wealth, of hidden kingdoms rich in gold and flowing with milk and honey. Joseph Banks, late of Cook's *Endeavour* voyage and now the unofficial impresario of British exploration, was too much a man of science to indulge either illusion, but ignorance of the "Dark Continent" was nevertheless the great "reproach upon the present age," he believed, and in 1788 he played the leading role in establishing the "Association for Promoting the Discovery of the Interior Parts of Africa," the first of several such bodies to evolve in time into the Royal Geographical Society. At its founding the African Association reflected a genuine interest in geographical knowledge for its own sake as well as a benevolent resolve to end the slave trade, but as time went on and evidence of French interest in the West African region grew, it became something like the stalking horse of empire, the benign face, as it were, of British commercial interests overseas.

Before Mungo Park appeared on the scene, the African Association had already sponsored three ill-fated incursions into the Niger region. Between the impenetrable growth, the torrid heat, the hostile tribes, and the pestilential atmosphere, the African interior presented challenges to exploration that Europeans had yet to face anywhere else in the world and before which they would regularly succumb throughout the nineteenth century. Park is a tragic case in point. His first expedition of 1795–96 succeeded insofar as against all odds, and in the face of tremendous human and environmental opposition, he actually found the Niger and returned home to tell about it.

Travels in the Interior Districts of Africa (1799), Park's riveting account of his first effort, was in fact a big best seller and one that set the survivalist standard for exploration narratives ever after. But his second effort in 1805 not only to find the Niger but to trace its course was a remorseless catalogue of disasters from start to finish; one by one the members of his escort either died, deserted, or went mad, leaving Park essentially alone to face the myriad hazards of the river. After seven months in the Senegambian wilderness, he set off from the Malian village of Sansanding resolved (as he put it in his last dispatch) "to discover the termination of the Niger or perish in the attempt," and perish he did, under mysterious circumstances, somewhere in the vicinity of the Bussa Rapids, some six hundred miles short of his obscure goal.

More even than Lewis and Clark, whose sense of adventure always stopped just short of recklessness and folly, it is Mungo Park, thoughtlessly sacrificing scores of men to his own personal and patriotic ambition, who announces a new style of exploration for a new colonial age. To be sure, some of its elements were old and familiar: in his cultural arrogance, his resort to violence, his susceptibility to fables, his lust for fame and fortune, Park harks back at least as far as the conquistadors. And there was nothing new in the link between exploration and empire, as the mere mention of the conquistadors proves. But the advent of a modern commercial and industrial economy in eighteenth-century Europe, and with it the modern nation-state, had altered the basis of colonial ambition and given it a nationalist edge it had lacked up to now. Bernal Díaz del Castillo spoke frankly for all the original conquistadors when he said he went to the Indies "both to serve God and our king and lord and to try to win honor, as noble men should do in life, and to go from good to better." Three centuries later, Mungo Park put the modern gloss on this when he spoke of "rendering the geography of Africa more familiar to my countrymen, and [of] opening to their ambition and industry new sources of wealth and new channels of commerce." And although he died without having realized either aim, his death secured his fame and eventually inspired other European explorers, other outriders of empire, to take up the dangerous African work that he had begun.

North and south

Meanwhile, British exploratory energies returned to a region that had teased the mercantile imagination since the days of John Cabot: the Canadian Arctic. All efforts to find the fabled Northwest Passage through those frigid waters had come to grief over the centuries, and George Vancouver tried to put the whole chimera to rest in 1798 when after six years of looking he emphatically declared that "no navigable communication whatever exists between the north pacific and north atlantic oceans." But dreams die hard, as Vancouver allowed. In 1816 the Baltic-born Russian explorer Otto von Kotzebue briefly thought he had found the passage at 67° north in the arm of the Chukchi Sea that now bears his name, and four years later his compatriots M. N. Vasil'ev and G. S. Shismarev took the search for it as far as Cook's "Icy Cape" on the Alaskan North Slope. Back in Great Britain, few still clung to the Elizabethan illusion that a passage, even if it existed, would be commercially useful. But national honor nevertheless demanded a response to these Russian overtures, or so at least John Barrow, the second secretary of the

Admiralty and in that capacity Joseph Banks's successor as the presiding genius of British exploration, successful argued. To have left the Northwest Passage "to be completed by a foreign navy after the doors of the two extremities had been thrown open by ships of our own," he wrote in patriotic reference to Cook and Baffin, "would have been little short of an act of national suicide; or, to say the least of it, an egregious piece of national folly."

And so what in retrospect looks like the even more egregious piece of national folly unfolded from 1818, when Barrow dispatched John Ross to find the Northwest Passage through Lancaster Sound, to 1848 when the twenty-four officers and 105 men of the John Franklin Expedition perished along with their ships somewhere in the vicinity of the Boothia Peninsula. The conditions the men of these successive expeditions endured as they overwintered, sick and starving, in these dark and frozen wastes defy description and do not admit of rational explanation. Scientific progress and national honor were the ostensible goals. Alongside these lay individual ambition and a desire to prove man's mastery over even the harshest of environments. But between the crisp lines of the official expedition accounts, with their high Victorian emphasis on noble sacrifice, the nature writer Barry Lopez rightly senses something more: a courage and determination so extreme as to seem eerie and peculiar rather than heroic. In place of a "resolute will before the menacing fortifications of the landscape"—the conventional reading of the record of Arctic exploration—Lopez finds a powerful human longing to achieve something significant, to transcend the self, "to be free of some of the grim weight of life." Of course this existential longing has a history going back to the earliest explorers. But in the Arctic it turned pathological. The Northwest Passage was a frozen mirage that men pursued "as if blinded by the snow and maddened by the ice."

Ever since Cook had circumnavigated the globe at 60° south and so disposed of the legend of Terra Australis, the Antarctic had held the British far less in thrall. Cook did not doubt there was land down there somewhere. But he reckoned its value at nil and so discouraged, for a time, any further thought of official Antarctic exploration. Unofficial exploration continued as sealers and whalers made their way farther and farther south in pursuit of ever-diminishing populations of prey, and in 1823 one of the sealers, James Weddell of Lanarkshire, surpassed even Cook's southernmost mark in the sea that now bears his name. This would never do. Exploration and discovery was a gentleman's game in the nineteenth century. For the obscure son of a Scottish upholsterer to hold the record of "farthest south" was no less a reproach to British dignity than for a foreigner to hold it, and through the 1820s and 1830s, as one whaler after another contributed one incidental discovery after another to an increasingly confused map of the Antarctic, the Admiralty began to wonder whether a renewal of Cook's effort were not necessary after all.

Fabian Gottlieb von Bellingshausen, another Baltic German in the service of Russia, completed a close circumnavigation of the Antarctic continent in 1820. He idolized Cook—not that that endeared him any to the British, who were quick to perceive here, as in the Arctic, a tsarist encroachment on their own territorial waters. The upstart Americans too were suddenly taking a jealous interest in the far south, as were those modern nationalists par excellence, the French, who were in fact especially eager to reclaim their naval honor and redeem the exploratory legacy of Bougainville. In each case, the preparatory work of proposal and persuasion, of outfitting and organization, took years. But by the late 1830s three full-blown naval and scientific expeditions, one British, one American, and one French, were converging on the Antarctic at once. The "race to the white continent" was on.

It ended, for now, in a much disputed draw. Although first on the scene, the French under the command of Jules Dumont d'Urville managed to get themselves ice-locked in the Weddell Sea and had to retreat for two years before returning to claim a barren rocky islet off the mainland at Terre Adélie in January 1840. By then, the Americans were also on the scene, and much controversy later surrounded the seemingly academic question of who had spotted the Antarctic mainland first. The American expedition, under the inept command of the mercurial Charles Wilkes, was a deadly disaster from start to finish. But before it ended in a welter of recrimination and courts martial, Wilkes had charted 1,500 miles of continuous frozen coastline, thus proving that Antarctica was a continental landmass and not a cluster of antipodal islands.

The British, last to arrive, left with the most to boast: a farthest south record of 74°23´ and the astonishing discovery of a 12,400-foot live volcano that the expedition's commander, James Clark Ross, named Mount Erebus, after his flagship. His main objective, the South Magnetic Pole, eluded him, but in the sea that now bears his name, Ross had more nearly approached it than anyone else by some hundreds of miles and, moreover, had also found what would ultimately prove the route of approach to the geographic pole itself. It was enough. When his attempt to sail even farther south in the Weddell Sea nearly ended in the loss of both of his ships the following season, Ross retreated, saying "he would not conduct another expedition to the South Pole for any money and a pension to boot."

"Dr. Livingstone, I presume"

James Clark Ross had good reasons for wanting to find the South Magnetic Pole in 1841. With the longitude puzzle finally solved, magnetism had emerged as the next great challenge not just to navigational science but to science in general, the key (or so Humboldt believed) to comprehending the cosmic unity of nature and the earth's geophysical laws. The British Association for the Advancement of Science, founded in 1831 to rival the stuffy amateurism of the Royal Society, made terrestrial magnetism an early priority and was the lead sponsor behind Ross's expedition:

publicly at least, his was a scientific mission in the Humboldtian mode. But it was also the elaborate expression of a personal ambition. Having already bagged the North Magnetic Pole in 1831 while accompanying his uncle's failed attempt on the Northwest Passage, Ross now wanted to capture its polar opposite. For a decade, he later said, he had cherished the hope "of being permitted to plant the flag of my country in both the magnetic poles of our globe."

Such a seemingly arbitrary ambition speaks to the changing nature of exploration in the age of empire. Explorers had always planted flags, of course, but usually on something they imagined to be of some godly or earthly use. Now the idea was to plant the flag of king and country on some remote extremity of no possible use, to be the first to stand on some objectively defined point of the earth's surface simply because it was there (as the British mountaineer George Mallory would later express it in accounting for his ambition to climb Mount Everest). The magnetic poles were a little unfulfilling in this respect for the simple reason that they moved around: they had a maddening tendency to migrate away from the spot where one had planted one's flag. The geographical poles were far worthier because fixed objectives, and they would soon enough absorb the rival ambitions of both individual explorers and nations. For now, however, with the poles still utterly inaccessible, some other prize would have to do, and of all the contenders, none loomed larger in the exploratory imagination than the source of the Nile River.

For more than two thousand years, ever since Aeschylus had written of an "Egypt nurtured by the snow," legend had associated the source of the Nile with an elusive range of central African mountains, Ptolemy's fabled "Mountains of the Moon." But European science generally dismissed such speculations until, in the late 1840s, German missionaries working out of Mombasa began to report distant sightings of snow-covered peaks. Even more intriguing were native reports of a vast inland sea in the same vicinity, and in 1856 the Royal Geographical Society—the institutional successor to Banks's African Association and now under the leadership of Sir Roderick Murchison, the world's "undisputed directorate of exploration"—dispatched Richard Burton, a veteran soldier-scholar-traveler with a self-professed mania for discovery, to the eastern interior to sort the whole puzzle out.

Working westward from Zanzibar along well-established slave caravan routes—here as elsewhere in Africa slavers were often the first explorers—Burton and his compatriot John Hanning Speke (along with their customarily large train of guides, interpreters, and porters) reached Lake Tanganyika in February 1858 only to find that, contrary to their hopes, it was not the source of the Nile. Leaving the malaria-stricken Burton to convalesce at Tabora, Speke reconnoitered ahead, stumbled unexpectedly on what he called Lake Victoria, and pronounced the problem solved. Refusing to cede the prize so easily, Burton expressed skepticism, and a bitter dispute followed that had the effect of riveting public attention on the Nile. When subsequent explorations by first, Speke, and then Samuel and Florence Baker failed fully to settle the issue, Murchison sent for an arbiter of unassailable authority: he sent for David Livingstone.

Born in a one-room tenement in the textile town of Blantyre, Scotland, in 1813, this most famous of nineteenth-century explorers had first gone to Africa as medical missionary in 1841, but almost from the moment he reached the London Missionary Society station of Kuruman, a then-remote oasis of the Kalahari, Livingstone's wanderlust ran ahead of his proselytizing purpose. "I view the end of the geographical feat as the beginning of the missionary enterprise," he wrote in *Missionary Travels and Researches in South Africa* (1857), his wildly popular account of his first sixteen years' residence in the "dark continent." It was the feat more than the enterprise that consumed him as he wandered ever deeper into the interior, ostensibly looking for a suitable site for a mission station but actually satisfying his restless curiosity and urge for discovery. His sighting of the Zambezi River in June 1851 encouraged his vision of a broad highway of "legitimate commerce" into regions still blighted by the slave trade, and one year later he returned to explore its upper reaches, always with the indispensable guidance and cooperation of the indigenous Makololo and other tribes. In May 1856, after years of harrowing travel, he succeeded in becoming the first European to traverse sub-Saharan Africa from coast to coast, the feat that together with his discovery of Victoria Falls made him famous and ensured a vast readership for his hastily produced memoir the following year.

Livingstone's second expedition to southeastern Africa, this time in the guise of a consular official charged with assessing the prospects for British trade in the interior, failed in every respect. The Zambezi turned out to be unnavigable, the plateau south of Lake Nyasa unsuited to missionary settlement, and Livingstone himself temperamentally wayward and diplomatically unreliable. But even failure could no longer diminish his standing in the eyes of the British establishment, and when public interest demanded a resolution to the mystery of the Nile, his return to Africa was inevitable. Setting out from Zanzibar in January 1866, accompanied this time only by African servants and porters, he so gave himself over to his uncommunicative wanderings that he led the outside world to believe he was dead or lost. He was neither. But in a move that speaks to the tight new relationship between exploration and popular journalism in the late nineteenth century, the *New York Herald*, sensing a scoop, dispatched the roving reporter Henry Morton Stanley to Africa under simple telegraphic orders to FIND LIVINGSTONE.

Thus the stage was set for one of the most famous episodes in the history of exploration, namely, the meeting of Stanley and Livingstone at Ujiji on November 10, 1871. In part it was Stanley's salutation—"Dr. Livingstone, I presume"—with its deliberate suggestion of gentlemanly insouciance in the wilderness, that immortalized the moment. Beyond that, something about the close juxtaposition of two such contrasting men—one saintly, austere, frail, and gentle; the other worldly, profligate, strong, and violent—caught the attention of posterity and lent the moment of their meeting an epochal significance. For Joseph Conrad, this was the moment that the disinterested quest for geographical knowledge gave way to an unholy scramble for wealth and territory. Livingstone, in Conrad's romantic imagination, was the last of the old heroic explorers, those "worthy, adventurous and devoted" men who nibbled at the edges, as he put it, "conquering a bit of truth here and a bit of truth there [until] swallowed up by the mystery their hearts were so persistently set on unveiling." Stanley, on the other hand, was the first of the new imperial breed, a tabloid reporter turned colonial mercenary whose African by-name of Bula Matari ("Breaker of Rocks") suggested a brutalist style of exploration that his critics still describe as "exploration by warfare." The contrast is overdrawn at both ends. Livingstone was never above a bit of rock breaking himself, and in his own pious way he was no less implicated than Stanley in the European colonial intrusion. Even so, a Bible is not the same thing as a bludgeon; a missionary is not the same thing as a soldier. At the end of the day, something fateful still hangs about this encounter on the shores of Lake Tanganyika, something ominous and portentous, as if one explorer had unwittingly drawn another to him and passed a torch from a restrained to a ruthless hand.

It adds to the ominous effect that Livingston had little time to live. Resisting Stanley's effort to extricate him from Africa, he carried on looking for the source of the Nile to the day of his death in 1873. Repatriated to England by two of his servants and buried in Westminster Abbey, he then became the totemic figure in the British colonial imagination, a martyr to the civilizing mission, the means by which the British linked antislavery and the Christian gospel to strategic and commercial interests, and so justified their African empire to themselves. Stanley, meanwhile, made

9. "Dr. Livingstone, I presume." One of many popular depictions of the somewhat staged meeting of Henry Morton Stanley and David Livingstone at Ujiji on the eastern shore of Lake Tanganyika, November 10, 1871.

internationally famous by his "finding" of Livingstone and subsequent circumnavigation of Lake Victoria, went on to carve out an empire in the Congo basin for King Leopold II of Belgium under the phony auspices of the International African Association. He ought not perhaps to be blamed for the subsequent atrocities that turned the Congo Free State into the ultimate charnel house of empire, but he was the explorer who more than any other touched off what came to be called the Scramble for Africa. If Mungo Park harked back to the conquistadors, Stanley simply became one and sealed the as yet uncertain link between exploration and empire.

Tournament of shadows

One year before Stanley and Livingstone's meeting at Ujiji, the great Russian explorer Nikolai Przhevalsky set out from the Siberian frontier outpost of Kiakhta on what proved to be the first of his four epic attempts to reach the "forbidden city" of Lhasa, some 1,600 miles to the south across the vast mountain-and-desert expanse of Mongolia and western China. Apart from one aimlessly wandering Englishman, Thomas Manning, in 1811, and two French Lazarist priests, Évariste Huc and Joseph Gabet in 1846, no westerner had entered Lhasa since the collapse of the Capuchin mission there in 1745. Lhasa had emerged as another great explorer's prize, less remote and inhospitable than the earth's poles or the source of the Nile, perhaps, but more fabled and alluring and geopolitically more sensitive. Though no Cibola or El Dorado, no mythic City of Gold, Lhasa was easily elided in western imaginings with Shambhala, the proverbial Asian paradise of peace and plenty. But it was also the actual capital of Tibet and thus a place of increasing strategic importance as three great empires, British, Russian, and Chinese, jealously converged on the Central Asian highlands. At one moment Przhevalsky was an explorer-pilgrim in search of Shangri-La; at another, he was an explorer-spy, the latest player in that long-standing contest for Central Asian hegemony that the British called "the Great Game" and the Russians "the Tournament of Shadows."

If Przhevalsky was the latest, the earliest notable player in the Tournament of Shadows was an English veterinary surgeon named William Moorcroft, who spent six years exploring the remote mountainous regions of Kashmir, Afghanistan, Turkistan, and Tibet before dying under mysterious circumstances returning from Bukhara in 1825. Ostensibly the superintendent of stud for the East India Company, Moorcroft was in fact an intelligence agent before the fact, the first wandering face of British anxiety over Russian encroachment on India. His death, however, proved the danger of deploying Europeans in a clandestine capacity in these perennially troubled regions; over time both the British and the Russians came to rely on native surrogates, Indians and Mongolians respectively, whom they trained in the combined arts of exploration and espionage and dispatched over the passes as the eyes and ears of empire. Thus, for instance, Nain Singh Rawat, a Bhotia schoolmaster in Kumaon whose languages included Hindi, Persian, English, and Tibetan, entered the pantheon of the great explorers as one of a hired corps of native surveyors who came to be known collectively as "the pundits," from the Sanskrit word for "learned one" or "scholar."

Starting from Kathmandu in the winter of 1866, Nain Singh (known to the British by his alias of "Pundit No. 1") crossed the Himalayan axis and surveyed eastward to Lhasa and then westward across the Tibetan plateau to the market town of Gartok at the foot of the Kailash Range. In a two-year journey of 1,500 miles, he fixed the course of the Brahmaputra River from its western source to Lhasa and also the positions and heights of countless Himalayan peaks. Two years later, he reached the fabled Thok-Jalung goldfields of western Tibet and traced the course of the Sutlej to the borders of British India. Here was a new phenomenon. Western explorers had almost always depended on native guidance to get them to where they were going. Nain Singh, though in the employ of the Raj, was a formidable explorer in his own right, as the Royal Geographical Society recognized in honoring him on his retirement in 1876 as "the man who has added a greater amount of positive knowledge to the map of Asia than any individual of our time."

By the time he retired, Nain Singh was one of about twenty native Indian explorers in the covert pay of the British Raj. His Russian-paid counterparts were never so many or well known. Nikolai Przhevalsky, on the other hand, though little remembered elsewhere, went on to become a Russian national hero of major proportions. He never did reach Lhasa. But in the course of four long expeditions between 1870 and 1887, he traversed more of the vast Central Asian plateau than any European before or possibly since. The Gobi Desert, the upper Yangtze, Eastern Turkistan and the Tian Shan, the Taklamakan Desert, the Tsaidam Basin, Dzungaria, and the Nan Shan: all *terra incognita* until Przhevalsky descended on it "with a carbine in one hand and a whip in the other," as he liked to say. Science was always part of his stated program, and the Russian Imperial Geographical Society duly honored Przhevalsky for his many topographical, botanical, and zoological discoveries (including that of his namesake horse).

But this was not the age of Enlightenment, and Przhevalsky was no Humboldt. He was a ruthless advocate of Russia's Asian destiny, one who in his last book proposed the wholesale removal of native Tibetans in favor of civilizing Cossacks. To Anton Chekhov, Przhevalsky represented a necessary antidote to sick and degenerate times. His "noble ambition" founded on love of country, his stubbornness, his undaunted urge to reach whatever goal he set himself, his immunity to heat, hunger, or fatigue, above all his "fanatical belief in Christian civilization and science"—all this, Chekhov wrote in an admiring obituary notice, made Przhevalsky a people's hero who personified a "higher moral force." To the British, though, it all made him a threat, and increasingly as the century wore on, they looked to counter his exploratory encroachments with some carbines and whips of their own.

And in the end it was the British who prevailed in the Tournament of Shadows, at least where the coveted prize of Lhasa was concerned. In 1903, alarmed at signs of amity between the Dalai Lama and the tsar, and maddened to distraction by Tibetan refusal to enter into trade relations, the pathologically Russophobic Indian viceroy, George Nathaniel Curzon, mounted a full-scale military mission under the command of Francis Edward Younghusband. Soldier, geographer, patriot, and mystic, Younghusband was the last great imperial adventurer, and he as much as Stanley or Przhevalsky evokes the essential colonial context of late-nineteenth-century exploration. The veteran already of an epic nineteen-month journey across Central Asia from Manchuria to Kashgar, he had also undertaken notable explorations of the High Pamirs and Karakoram and was the first European to cross the Himalayan axis from the Xinjiang region of China to Kashmir. Whether such exploratory feats and the honor of the Founder's Medal of the Royal Geographical Society qualified him to lead a military mission to Tibet one might well doubt, and indeed Younghusband made a bloody mess of it, massacring as he went and dramatically worsening Anglo-Tibetan relations. But the prize at least was his, as on August 3, 1904, the gilded roofs of the Potala Palace came into view and the Forbidden City was "finally unveiled" (as the tabloid press had it).

Alas, no Shambhala as it turned out, Lhasa was (apart from the splendid Potala) a perfectly ordinary place, squalid and dismal even in the eyes of its invaders, and when Younghusband failed to find any Russians lurking about, London grew restive, recalled the mission, and effectively disowned the punitive convention that he had imposed at bayonet point. Though not clear at the time, the tide of empire had finally turned, and a long era ended. For Tibet was the last thickly settled place of any importance to defy European intrusion, and in forcing its gates the Younghusband Mission unconsciously closed out the high colonial chapter in the history of western exploration.

Chapter 7
To the ends of the earth

In every end is a beginning, of course; every epilogue is prologue. With the filling of the large space on the map that was Tibet and High Asia, explorers turned to smaller spaces, to the infinite recesses between and among the routes of cultural convergence that explorers had traced to date, or else they turned to those untouched extremities where there was no map, where there were no cultures, where vast emptiness of earth and sky was itself the beckoning allure. Of the latter, of those last empty and unvisited immensities, none inspired more turn-of-the-century fascination than the Arctic and the Antarctic. The unveiling of Lhasa may have ended one familiar form of western exploration. But with the impending race to the poles, north and south, another was set to begin; five centuries after Columbus, the very ends of the earth were finally within human reach.

The Arctic grail

In the Arctic, polar exploration was a natural extension of the quest for the Northwest Passage that had occupied European powers since the Age of Discovery. The disappearance of the Franklin Expedition in 1847 had finally dampened British enthusiasm for the passage, but national honor nevertheless demanded an effort at rescue of any possible survivors, and so, in one of the odder chapters of exploration history, Franklin himself became the object of the quest, the focus of some forty-two increasingly desperate relief expeditions between 1847 and 1879. When one of these turned up evidence that Franklin's men had been driven to cannibalism in their effort to survive, the reaction in Great Britain was electric. Arctic exploration was supposed to reflect the high moral and supremely civilized character of the British race: that it instead had evidently led to the ultimate measure of primitive degradation was both humbling and not a little titillating. Once having taken this turn for the macabre, the search for Franklin seized the public imagination as the quest for the Northwest Passage never had and altered the basis of Arctic exploration. Where once the whole point had been to get through the frozen archipelago to somewhere else, now the point was to linger and see what the region itself had to offer, either in terms of Franklin relics or, failing those, all-purpose geographic or ethnographic interest. By 1850 the Arctic had become an important region in its own right, and from this newfound importance came the thought of a journey to the pole, the ultimate and inevitable end of all earthly ambition.

Among the first to make an outright attempt on the North Pole was the American newspaper publisher Charles Francis Hall, whose journalistic interest in the Franklin story had led him to mount two rescue missions of his own—one to Baffin Island and one to King William Island—in the 1860s. What distinguished these from the many others to date was Hall's explicit embrace of Inuit wisdom as the key to Arctic travel and survival. Where earlier explorers had both artfully concealed their dependence on the native Inuit and kept themselves at a disdainful distance from those they regarded as savages, Hall purposefully "went native," as the contemporary expression held, and made cultural encounter and adaptation the very basis of his long residence in the Arctic. He never found Franklin, but his "life among the Esquimaux" (to borrow from the title of his pioneering ethnography of 1864) eventually encouraged his ambition of becoming the first man to stand directly under Polaris, the "crowning jewel," as he described it, "of the Arctic dome."

Sadly, Hall's single attempt on the North Pole ended in equal parts tragedy and ignominy when Hall himself died of arsenic poisoning (under mysterious and possibly murderous circumstances), and most of his company ended up marooned and adrift on the ice floes of Smith Sound. The British briefly reentered the fray in 1875 with an expedition under George Strong Nares that, if nothing else, effectively disproved the antique notion of an open polar sea by dispatching men across frozen water to a then-record latitude of 83°20′ north. Thereafter, the Arctic became a distinctly American stage, one on which a still-young nation both asserted its manhood and tried to address its collective ambivalence toward progress.

Cosmopolitan science made one last stand in 1881, when Adolphus Greely led an ostensible research expedition to Ellesmere Island under the coordinated auspices of the first International Polar Year. But no sooner had the team of two dozen soldiers and two Greenland Inuit arrived at Lady Franklin Bay than "farthest north" emerged as Greely's true priority. Owing to a combination of poor planning and poor judgment, the expedition ended in the loss of eighteen men to starvation and exposure, and thus science and polar exploration parted company for a while. Heroic sacrifice was now the thing—exertion, struggle, agony. And if a bit of murder and mayhem attached to it, as was the case with both the Hall and Greely expeditions, well so much the better from the point of view of newspaper editors. Tragedy sold, or so it seemed in the aftermath of Greely's rescue. And though Greely himself was too frail and refined a person to play the role of explorer-hero to perfection, his expedition nevertheless marked a crucial stage toward defining it. Henceforth, the polar explorer had to conform to an atavistic ideal of manliness and set his bold and rugged face not just against the worst that nature had to offer but against the comfort and decadence of an overcivilized age.

There was, certainly, an alternative style of polar exploration that far from shunning the advances of civilization embraced them as the means to success. Thus in 1906 the journalist Walter Wellman, having twice failed to reach the pole by the traditional means of boat and dog-sled, decided to go there by motorized airship. "The time has come to adopt new methods, to make an effort to substitute modern science for brute force," he insisted, and though his own effort at such substitution ended in failure when the forty-horsepower engines of his colossal 185-foot dirigible *America* proved no match for Arctic winds, his technological vision lived on and ultimately triumphed when it came to the exploration of space, obviously, or the deep ocean. For now, however, the antitechnological and antimodern ethos, the idea of exploration as the purposeful pursuit of the primitive held sway and found its embodiment in the uniquely persistent figure of Robert Peary, an American naval engineer whose twenty-year effort on the North Pole ultimately reduced to the twin essentials, as he once put it, of "man and the Eskimo dog."

Peary's chief rival through the long years of his Arctic odyssey was the great Norwegian explorer Fridtjof Nansen, who by a deft combined use of Nordic skis and light sleds—the latter inspired by Inuit design—achieved the first known crossing of Greenland from Angmagssalik to Godthåb Fjord in 1888, thus stealing a march on Peary's first intention. Five years later, in one of the most stirring feats of courageous intelligence in the history of arctic exploration, Nansen very nearly bagged the pole by deliberately running his purpose-built ship *Fram* into the ice in the vicinity of the New Siberian Islands, drifting with the pack as far north as it would take him, and then making a dogsled dash from the ship for the final prize. He fell short by 225 miles, but at 86°14′ he was farther north than anyone had ever been and would return to Norway a national celebrity and a goad to Robert Peary's sharply competitive ambition.

Whether Peary's ambition and lust for glory, together with a reckless series of mercenary obligations to his sponsors, led him ultimately to falsify a claim to the North Pole is one of the great open questions in the history of exploration. The story as Peary presented it to the public was that from a winter camp at Cape Sheridan on the north coast of Ellesmere Island, he and his support crew of twenty-one Americans and some one hundred Inuit set out for the pole in relay stages at the end of February 1909. A month later, at 87°47′ north and 133 geographical miles from the pole, Peary inexplicably dismissed his navigator, Captain Bob Bartlett, and carried on with four native Inuit and Matthew Henson, his long-time African American servant and fellow explorer. On April 6, according to Peary's own astronomical calculations, "the prize of 3 centuries" fell to him. "The Pole at last!!!" he exulted in his journal. "My dream and goal for 23 years MINE at last." How galling it must have been then to arrive back at the settlement of Etah to the news that Frederick Cook, an American rival well known to Peary from earlier shared expeditions, had in the meantime shown up in Annoatak claiming to have reached the pole a year earlier and was now en route to a royal reception and international acclaim in Copenhagen.

The ensuing controversy, the Cook-Peary controversy as it came to be called, has never been settled and points to the often subjective and arbitrary quality of "discovery" in the age of extremes. The geographical poles are very real, of course; they exist in both a concrete and abstract sense, but they are (or at least were) difficult to locate with perfect precision. In the absence of obviously identifying features or reliably corroborative testimony—and in 1909 neither African Americans nor native Inuit qualified in white minds as reliable—the public had to take the explorer's claims to have reached them on faith. Conflicting claims had to be judged on the basis of character or just deserts, and never was this more the case than with Cook and Peary, neither one of whom could offer any objective proof of having reached the North Pole. After brief acclaim, Cook emerged as an obvious fraud, one who had already faked a first ascent of Alaska's Mount McKinley, and so the nod went to the more established, respectable, and officially sponsored Peary almost by default. Contemporary doubts about his claim have only grown over time, however, and though both men have their defenders still, the gathering consensus is that neither reached the pole.

Does that matter at all? Disputes over priority and faked claims would seem to have little real bearing on the history of exploration. On the other hand, priority, being first, is what exploration is fundamentally about, especially where nothing else is at stake, and we should not wonder that the Cook-Peary controversy continues to sustain a robust forensic literature. Its short-term effect, meanwhile, the savage virulence with which Peary especially conducted his campaign of discrediting Cook, was to bring the work of exploration into general ill-repute. It needed a martyr to redeem it, and it soon enough found one in the irreproachable and romantically named figure of Robert Falcon Scott.

The last place on earth

In the late-nineteenth and early-twentieth centuries, the high drama of polar exploration played itself out largely in the Arctic. For whatever reason, the Antarctic did not then seize the public imagination in quite the same way; it lacked what contemporaries referred to as the glamour of the north. This was bound to change, however, once the South Pole earned its status as the earth's last virgin prize, and indeed, even before Cook and Peary lay their competing claims to 90° north, 90° south had begun to recover some of the allure that it had held a century earlier, when the fact of an antipodal landmass was still barely known. In 1893 Sir Clements Markham, a veteran of the midcentury search for Franklin and a long-time champion of British polar exploration, acceded to the presidency of the Royal Geographical Society and vigorously directed its lobbying energies toward true south. He tactfully disavowed any nationalist interest in doing so and graciously played host when in 1895 the Sixth International

Geographical Congress officially urged Antarctic exploration on governments and scientific societies throughout the world. Yet for all his public embrace of the cosmopolitan calling of science for its own sake, Markham thought of the Antarctic as a natural extension of Great Britain's empire and a worthy ground on which to perform deeds of colonial derring-do. Never mind practical benefits. It was the purity of the quest that captivated him, the chance it offered the youth of England to test their chivalric mettle against the frozen elements.

Markham cannot have been pleased, then, when a Belgian expedition under Adrien de Gerlache overwintered in the Bellingshausen Sea and thus inaugurated the heroic age of Antarctic exploration in 1898. The next in the lists, the Norwegian-born schoolmaster Carsten Borchgrevink, was reassuringly half-English, and his backer (the magazine magnate Sir George Newnes) wholly so, but Markham nevertheless resented his private trespass on the august authority of the Royal Geographical Society and was pleased when Borchgrevink's self-styled "British Antarctic Expedition" achieved little beyond a new "farthest south" of 78°50´ in February 1900. By then, Markham's own "British National Antarctic Expedition" had come together under the formidable auspices of the RGS, the Royal Society, the Admiralty, and the Royal Navy. It had a specially built polar research ship, the first of its kind, in RRS *Discovery* and as of May 1900 an officially sanctioned leader in Commander Robert Scott.

By his own admission, Scott had no predilection for polar exploration when he became the British face of it, nor any experience of independent command. But he was young, charming, and charismatic—qualities that Markham valued above experience. He had an appropriately scientific turn of mind. Above all, he had a suitably romantic and heroic conception of exploration that found expression, for instance, in his famously perverse preference for man-hauling over dogs. "In my mind," he wrote, "no journey ever made with dogs can approach the height of that fine conception which is realized when a party of men go forth to face hardships, dangers, difficulties with their own unaided efforts, and by days and weeks of hard physical labour succeed in solving some problem of the great unknown. Surely in this case the conquest is more nobly and splendidly won." Or if not, he might have added, then nobly and splendidly lost, for Scott defines that type of gentleman-explorer for whom the "fine conception" mattered more than the end result, and death itself seemed preferable to success by unsporting or unchivalrous means.

From a base on Ross Island at the edge of the enormous frozen barrier now known as the Ross Ice Shelf, Scott's *Discovery* expedition of 1901–4 undertook the first systematic exploration of the Antarctic interior. The company included Edward Wilson, who besides being a reckonable surgeon and ornithologist has the distinction of being among the last expeditionary artists— photography now coming into its own as the explorer's visual medium of choice—and one Lieutenant Ernest Shackleton, late of the merchant marine, who would soon emerge as a formidable rival to Scott's polar ambitions. For now, however, Scott and Shackleton worked in reasonable harmony and together with Wilson achieved a new "farthest south" of 82°17′ before depleted provisions and the specter of scurvy forced a halt on December 30, 1902. The following spring, Scott led an even more impressive sledding journey up the Farrar Glacier and westward along the 9,000-foot polar plateau for a then-record distance of 200 miles. On the whole, the *Discovery* expedition successfully fulfilled its ambitious dual program of scientific research and geographical discovery and emphatically confirmed Scott in his anointed role as Great Britain's Antarctic ambassador.

Even so, in 1907 a glory-seeking Ernest Shackleton stole a march on his old commander and led a private expedition that came within one hundred miles of the pole before turning back at a new record latitude of 88°23′ S. The prize of centuries was close at hand, and when in 1909 the North Pole seemingly fell to the

Americans, the pressure on Scott to claim it for the glory of Great Britain mounted tremendously. It still would not do to make an outright dash for the pole, however: no honor or dignity in that. And so the second of Scott's polar expeditions, the ill-fated *Terra Nova* expedition of 1910–12, was once again a large and cumbersome affair designed as much for a leisurely program of scientific research as for an assault on the pole. "We want the scientific work to make the bagging of the pole merely an item in the results," is how Edward Wilson put it, and it was with this somewhat muddled but gentlemanly sense of purpose that the expedition sailed from Cardiff on June 15, 1910. Four months saw it to Melbourne, where on October 12 Scott received an unsettlingly cryptic telegram that read: "Beg leave to inform you *Fram* proceeding Antarctic. Amundsen."

"Amundsen" was Roald Engelbregt Gravning Amundsen, a name to conjure with and one inseparably joined to Scott's in historical myth and memory. At age thirty-eight, Amundsen too was a veteran of the Antarctic, having been with the Belgians in the Bellingshausen Sea in 1898–99, but his claim to fame lay on his successful transit of the Northwest Passage beginning in 1903. Here he demonstrated all the qualities that were make him so formidable a rival to Scott: his innate feel for ice and snow, his ability on skis, his understanding of the essential role of dogs in polar travel, his willingness to learn from the native Inuit and adapt their practices to his own, and, above all, his appreciation of the need to think small and travel light where Arctic exploration was concerned. Where the British had customarily attempted the Northwest Passage in heavily manned naval vessels of three hundred tons or more, Amundsen did it with a crew of six on a forty-five-ton herring sloop. To the British, this hardly counted, and some conspicuous time passed before the Royal Geographical Society begrudgingly conferred its patron's medal on Amundsen in 1907. But to the Norwegians, newly independent of Sweden as they were, Amundsen became a founding national hero. With the blessing and support of the great Fridtjof Nansen—who now put the *Fram* at his disposal—Amundsen next set his sights on the North Pole, abruptly and secretly changing his plans only when he learned of first Cook's and then Peary's purported success. What qualm of conscience led him to alert Scott to his true intentions in October 1912 (when it was already too late for Scott to make any substantial changes to his expedition design or itinerary) is unclear. But from that moment, the famous "race to the pole" was on, and its outcome virtually ordained.

For his part, Scott, knowing that he could not compete on equal terms for speed and unwilling, perhaps, to take too much notice of one he regarded as an interloper and base record chaser, refused to be drawn into a race and affirmed that his largely scientific show would go on as planned. And so from opposite ends of the Ross Ice Shelf a fascinating study in contrasts played out between the last of the old-style colonial expeditions in all its lumbering comprehensiveness and the first of the new style of professional expeditions in all its efficient single-mindedness. That the race stayed as near-run a thing as it did is, in retrospect, remarkable; had Scott not been dogged by particular misfortune especially where weather was concerned, he might well have claimed the South Pole for king and country after all. As it happened, with Amundsen making an astounding twenty-five miles a day on skis and dogsleds, Scott lost by about a month and had to console himself that he and his four companions (as one of them put it in his diary) had "done it by good British man-hauling," that theirs was "the greatest journey done by man unaided."

Science too redeemed the defeat, or so Scott seemed intent to prove even amidst the most harrowing and hard-pressed retreat in the history of extreme exploration. When Scott's life and the lives of four others hung precariously in the balance, he took precious time and energy out to gather thirty-five pounds of rock samples from the moraines of the Beardmore Glacier. Amundsen would not have these to show. Or was this geological dalliance not so much an effort to salvage scientific meaning for the expedition as

10. The perils of polar exploration: Robert Falcon's Scott's expedition ship *Terra Nova* icebound in the Antarctic, 1910 or 1911.

a conscious form of suicide, a way of ensuring that Scott and his companions would die their martyrs' deaths just eleven poignant miles from the depot of their salvation? We will never know. "Had we lived, I should have had a tale to tell of the hardihood,

110

endurance, and courage of my companions which would have stirred the heart of every Englishman," Scott scrawled in his last wrenching "Message to the Public," and in the end it was not science but the dignity of his death that redeemed the expedition in the eyes of a mournful public. Amundsen may have bagged the pole, but Scott had gone south "to prove once again that the manhood of our nation is not dead and that the characteristics of our ancestors who won our great Empire still flourish amongst us," as Major Leonard Darwin, the president of the Royal Geographical Society, had earlier put it. Soon enough, the hideous carnage of the Great War would discredit such pompous imperial posturing, and Scott would come to be seen as an incompetent bungler who had no business being in the Antarctic in the first place. For now, however, as "Scott of the Antarctic," he perfectly reflected the arrogance of his age and by the grand manner of his dying lent "the last place on earth" a heroic aura it has never completely lost.

Because it's there

"The whole world has now been discovered," wrote a correspondent for the *New York Times* on hearing of Amundsen's attainment of the South Pole, and so it must have seemed to a generation that had come to think of 90° latitude as the ultimate pinnacle of exploratory achievement. But latitude is only one of many possible ways in which to define the earth's geographical extremities. Altitude is another, and in retrospect it is not surprising that once the poles had fallen, the world's highest mountain emerged as the great remaining terrestrial prize. To be sure, Himalayan exploration had its own long history reaching far back into the colonial era. But only after Peary and Amundsen had won the poles for lesser upstart powers did the British begin to style Mount Everest "the third pole" and make it the focus of determined expeditionary effort. It was in this context that George Leigh Mallory—the climber who would soon join Robert Scott in the revered company of martyrs to pointless courage—coined the epigraph to modern exploration when, in reply to a reporter who asked why he wanted to climb Mount Everest, he quipped, "Because it's there." Amundsen might have said the same thing about the South Pole, and indeed, sensational achievement for its own sake had long been coming to the fore of the exploratory mind-set. But Mallory's quip captured this truth more succinctly than anything else had done and so set the tone for the rest of the century. Explorers, as the French mountain climber Lionel Terray expressed it, were now *"les conquérant de l'inutile,"* the conquistadors of the useless.

Not that the opportunities for exploration as traditionally conceived in strategic, scientific, or commercial terms were completely exhausted. Consider a few random examples drawn from the period following the race to the poles: in 1913–14, with war in Europe and Ottoman Arabia impending, the redoubtable Gertrude Bell undertook a hazardous expedition from Damascus into the little-known heart of the Nafud Desert on behalf of British intelligence; in 1924–25, a latter-day Humboldt named Frank Kingdon-Ward led a botanical expedition into the remote recesses of the Tsangpo Gorges in southeastern Tibet; and in 1930 an Australian freebooter named Michael Leahy went looking for gold and found, to his great surprise, people in what he expected to be the uninhabited interior of highland New Guinea. Thus the age-old motives endured. George Mallory may have wanted to climb Everest simply because it was there, but the expeditions he joined in the 1920s were large and traditionally conceived affairs combining all sorts of colonial, scientific, and commercial purposes. Robert Scott far more than Roald Amundsen was their conceptual inspiration.

Still, as the twentieth century proceeded and the public taste for sensation intensified, adventure for its own sake—the stunt, the splash, the "next big thing"—undeniably eclipsed worthier goals as traditionally construed. Denied the South Pole, Ernest Shackleton thus set out to be the first to cross the entirety of the Antarctic continent in 1914. Having bagged the Northwest Passage and the South Pole, Amundsen set out to be the first to fly an airplane over the North Pole in 1926. It was the age of showmanship: the travel writer Peter Fleming understood as much as early as 1933 when he wrote that adventure in the "grand old manner" was obsolete and that to make one's mark as an explorer today one had to undertake an exploit "at once highly improbable and absolutely useless," like "driving a well-known make of car along the Great Wall of China in reverse."

This was not quite fair. If the age of geographical discovery had gone, as Fleming claimed it had, if he himself could claim nothing but the discovery of "one new tributary to a tributary to a tributary of the Amazon," there were still a few unvisited corners of the world, and of these none loomed larger now than the Rub' al Khali, the "Empty Quarter," those 250,000 miles of parched desert in southeastern Arabia that T. E. Lawrence once called "the last unwritten plot of earth." The British Arabist Bertram Thomas had crossed it quickly and obliquely 1930–31 as had his compatriot Harry St. John Philby in 1932. But the "spirit of the Empty Quarter" was Wilfred Thesiger, who in the trusted and indispensable company of the Rashid Bedouin made the first sustained journeys through its endlessly drifting sands in the years following the Second World War. "Journeying at walking pace under conditions of some hardship, I was perhaps the last explorer in the tradition of the past," Thesiger wrote in his autobiography, and while much hangs on the qualifier, "perhaps," he generally deserves his Eurocentric reputation as "the first man to the last places." A few scraps of unexplored earth remained and always will, but the Rub' al Khali was the "last great blank on the map," as the traditional turn of phrase has it, and with its filling in the so-called "heroic age" of exploration had certifiably ended.

Epilogue: Final frontiers?

In the winter of 1942/43, in Nazi-occupied Paris, Émile Gagnan and a ship-of-the-line lieutenant named Jacques-Yves Cousteau together developed the first modern prototype of the Aqua-Lung, or "self-contained underwater breathing apparatus" (SCUBA). Various sorts of diving bells and chambers had been around since the Renaissance, and in 1930 two Americans, William Beebe and Otis Barton, had made history's first deep-sea descent off Bermuda in a hollow steel ball they called a bathysphere. But it was the Gagnan-Cousteau Aqua-Lung, allowing as it did for free range of movement, observation, and collection, that ushered in the brave new era of undersea exploration. In 1948, while Wilfred Thesiger was making his second crossing of the Empty Quarter in Arabia, Cousteau and a small team that included the explorer-photographer Marcel Ichac made autonomous diving excavations of the ancient Mediterranean shipwreck of Mahdia, thus opening the way for submarine archaeology. Two years later, having resigned his naval commission, Cousteau founded French Oceanographic Campaigns, converted a retired British minesweeper into the research vessel *Calypso*, and set out on his lifelong career as the world's leading apostle of underwater discovery. The waters that compass us about, he wrote in 1959, are "the last frontier on our planet," and to him they presented a challenge "larger and more mysterious than the terrestrial wilderness, the deserts, the peaks and the white wastes of the Poles."

In writing thus of "the last frontier on our planet," Cousteau acknowledged that others off our planet now beckoned, that the lowly earth could no longer contain human exploratory ambition. Two years before he wrote, the Soviet Union had successfully placed an artificial satellite, *Sputnik 1*, into elliptical low earth orbit, and two years after that, the Soviet pilot Yuri Gagarin became the first human to journey beyond the earth's atmosphere into interplanetary space. A scant half-century after the race to the poles, the Cold War–inspired race to the moon was on.

But was Gagarin actually an explorer in the same sense as Peary or Amundsen or their many earth-bound predecessors? Not once during his seventy-nine-minute near-orbit of the earth on April 12, 1961, did Gagarin touch the controls of his *Vostok* spacecraft. More passenger than pilot, he was simply along for the ride, a bit of flesh-and-blood cargo on an otherwise purely robotic and technologically driven venture. Subsequent cosmonauts and American astronauts had marginally more direct responsibility for the course and bearing of their crafts (from lunar landers to low-orbit shuttles), but still very little, none practically, compared with that of Columbus or Cook for theirs. And while space travel is unquestionably dangerous, as the American shuttle disasters prove, those who undertake it do not leap off into the unknown as daringly as the Vikings or Polynesians did. Rather, they set out on minutely programmed and computer-controlled courses for precisely fixed and perfectly located destinations. That is, they know to a scientific certainty where they are going and how long it will take them to get there. If the explorer by very definition has no precise or known destination, then astronauts are not explorers.

But neither, then, were Peary and Amundsen, both of whom had the mathematically precise destination of 90° latitude in mind when they set out on their polar journeys. And although they both had to rely far more on their own human energies and instincts to get there than Neil Armstrong had to rely on his to get to the Sea of Tranquility on the Moon, they too had technological tools at their disposal that earlier polar travelers did not and might thus be disqualified by absolute purists from the company of explorers. True, technology stifles romance, and by comparison with those earlier explorers who did not know what was over the next hill or around the next bend in the river, astronauts seem terribly spoiled. But so then does James Cook by comparison with the Polynesians who navigated the same seas without benefit of ship or sextant or magnetic compass. The differences here are matters of degree, not of kind. The real question is not how one travels but whether one travels to find the new. The point of the explorer's journey is to see what has not been seen by anyone before, and in that respect no one in history was more of an explorer than Yuri Gagarin, who was the first human to see the bright blue orb of the earth set against the deep black immensity of space.

Is space then "the final frontier," as the famous title sequence to the 1960s television series *Star Trek* has it? If so, then it is an infinitely expanding one, and the work of exploration will never end as long as human curiosity endures. The particular geopolitical rivalry that drove the race to the moon ended with the Cold War, and the commercial usefulness of space travel has yet to prove itself as has the ambassadorial: we have yet to make any form of cultural contact out there.

In other cultural and psychological respects, however, the exploration of space represents the deep extension of tendencies already evident in the earliest human migrations. The Romantics called it "wanderlust"—this innate human instinct for travel and original experience, this indefinable urge to see what lies over the next ridge or ocean. But it may be something more deeply wired than that. In looking into the riddle of human restlessness—no other mammal moves around from choice like we do—evolutionary anthropologists have identified a variant of the *DRD4* gene, namely *DRD4-7R*, that in fact disposes some 20 percent of us toward curiosity, risk, movement, and adventure.

11. The final frontier? American astronaut Edwin E. "Buzz" Aldrin Jr. at Tranquility Base, the Moon, July 21, 1969. The photo was taken by Neil Armstrong, who appears reflected in Aldrin's visor along with the Apollo 11 Lunar Module *Eagle*.

There is no such thing as the explorer's gene: that vastly overstates 7R's determinative significance. In accounting for the mystery of human exploration one has to consider means as much as motives, the ability as much as the urge. But where the urge is concerned, the familiar trinity of God, Gold, and Glory does not, it appears, tell the whole story. We need another "G" for Genes to explain why for thousands of years *Homo sapiens*, the "wise human," has wandered the earth as *Homo explorans*.

"I suppose we go to Mount Everest," George Mallory once said, "because—in a word—we can't help it." He spoke more truth than he knew. For all the different forms it takes in different historical periods, for all the worthy and unworthy motives that lie behind it, exploration, travel for the sake of discovery and adventure, seems to be a human compulsion, a human obsession even (as the paleontologist Maeve Leakey says); it is a defining element of a distinctly human identity, and it will never rest at any frontier, whether terrestrial or extraterrestrial.

Space that is to say (with all due respect to Captain Kirk) is not the final frontier. Submarine and subterranean exploration are only just beginning. Vast stretches of the Arctic and Antarctic remain unvisited and unexplored. By some alarmist estimates, we are losing an acre of tropical rainforest approximately every second, but where it survives, the rainforest remains a space of infinite and impenetrable mystery. We have mapped every inch of the geosphere, but we have scarcely touched the biosphere. According to one recent estimate, even in this age of mass extinctions, 86 percent of the earth's 8.7 million species remain unknown to science. And remarkably enough, there are even some people still out there to be found. As of January 2007, Brazil's National Indian Foundation confirmed the presence of sixty-seven officially "uncontacted" tribes in the Amazonian interior. Once they have all succumbed to the appropriative gaze of the outside world, the history of exploration as human encounter will finally have ended. And then we will see what other form of exploratory encounter awaits, whether in this world, some other, or the next.

References

Chapter 1: What is (and is not) exploration?

Encarta Webster's Dictionary of the English Language, 2nd ed. (New York: Bloomsbury, 2004), s.v. "exploration."

Oxford English Dictionary, 2nd ed. (Oxford: Clarendon Press, 2005), s.v. "exploration," "explore."

Paul Carter, *The Road to Botany Bay* (Chicago: University of Chicago Press, 1987), 26.

Joseph Conrad, "Geography and Some Explorers," *National Geographic* 45, no. 3 (1924).

Ralph Waldo Emerson, *The Complete Works*, vol. 11 (Boston: Houghton, Mifflin, 1904), 457.

Chapter 2: The peopling of the earth

J. C. Beaglehole, ed., *The Journals of Captain James Cook on His Voyages of Discovery*, vol. 3 (Cambridge: Cambridge University Press, 1961), 279.

James Cook and James King, *A Voyage to the Pacific Ocean Undertaken by the Command of His Majesty for Making Discoveries in the Northern Hemisphere*, vol. 1 (London: G. Nichol, 1784), 200–202.

Magnus Magnusson and Hermann Pálsson, eds., *The Vinland Sagas: The Norse Discovery of America* (London: Penguin, 1965), 54.

Chapter 3: First forays

Daniel Boorstin, *The Discoverers* (New York: Random House, 1983), 99.

Felipe Fernández-Armesto, *Columbus* (Oxford: Oxford University Press, 1991), 188.

H. A. R. Gibb, *Ibn Batutta: Travels in Asia and Africa* (London: Routledge, 1929), 12.

Robin Hanbury-Tenison, ed., *The Oxford Book of Exploration* (Oxford: Oxford University Press, 1993).

Chapter 4: The age of exploration

Christopher Columbus, *Journal of the First Voyage*, ed. and trans. B. W. Ife (Warminster: Aris & Phillips, 1990), v, 5.

J. H. Parry, *The Age of Reconnaissance* (New York: Mentor, 1963), 50, 55.

Adam Smith, *An Inquiry into the Nature and Causes of the Wealth of Nations*, vol. 2 (London: W. Strahan, 1778), 237.

Chapter 5: Exploration and the Enlightenment

Charlotte Barrett, ed., *Diary and Letters of Madame d'Arblay*, vol. 1 (London: Macmillan, 1904), 318.

J. C. Beaglehole, ed., *The Journals of Captain James Cook on His Voyages of Discovery*, vol. 2 (Cambridge: Cambridge University Press, 1961), 175, 643.

Alex Calder, Jonathan Lamb, and Bridget Orr, eds., *Voyages and Beaches* (Honolulu: University of Hawai'i Press, 1999), 101.

Neil Safier, *Measuring the New World: Enlightenment Science and South America* (Chicago: University of Chicago Press, 2008), 18.

Laura Dassow Walls, *The Passage to Cosmos: Alexander Humboldt and the Shaping of America* (Chicago: University of Chicago Press, 2009), 19.

Chapter 6: Exploration and empire

John Barrow, *Voyages of Discovery and Research within the Arctic Regions* (London: John Murray, 1846), 16.

Frank Bergon, ed., *The Journals of Lewis and Clark* (New York: Penguin, 1995), xxv–xxvi.

Bernal Díaz del Castillo, *The True History of the Conquest of New Spain*, trans. Janet Burke and Ted Humphrey (Indianapolis: Hackett, 2012), 6.

Joseph Conrad, "Geography and Some Explorers," in *Last Essays*, ed. Harold Ray Stevens, J. H. Stape, and Owen Knowles (Cambridge: Cambridge University Press, 2010), 3–17.

John Gascoigne, *Science in the Service of Empire: Joseph Banks, the British State and the Uses of Science in the Age of Revolution* (Cambridge: Cambridge University Press, 1998), 179.

David Livingstone, *Missionary Travels and Researches in South Africa* (New York: Harper, 1870), 718.

Barry Lopez, *Arctic Dreams: Imagination and Desire in a Northern Landscape* (New York: Charles Scribner's Sons, 1986), 308, 310.

Karl E. Meyer and Shareen Blair Brysac, *Tournament of Shadows: The Great Game and the Race for Empire in Central Asia* (Washington, DC: Counterpoint, 1999), 232, 240, 299.

Mungo Park, *The Journal of a Mission to the Interior of Africa in the year 1805* (Philadelphia: Edward Earle, 1815), 76.

James Clark Ross, *A Voyage of Discovery and Research in the Southern and Antarctic Regions During the Years 1839–43* (London: John Murry, 1847), 246.

Robert A. Stafford, "Scientific Exploration and Empire," in *The Oxford History of the British Empire*, vol. 3, ed. Andrew Porter (Oxford: Oxford University Press, 1999), 297.

George Vancouver, *A Voyage of Discovery to the North Pacific Ocean*, vol. 3 (London: G. G. and J. Robinson, 1798), 500.

Chapter 7: To the ends of the earth

David Crane, *Scott of the Antarctic: A Biography* (London: HarperCollins, 2005), 398.

C. H. Davis, ed., *Narrative of the North Polar Expedition* (Washington, DC: Government Printing Office, 1876), 19.

Peter Fleming, *Brazilian Adventure* (New York: Charles Scribner's Sons, 1934), 6, 28–29.

Roland Huntford, *Scott and Amundsen* (New York: G. P. Putnam's Sons, 1980), 317.

L. Huxley, ed., *Scott's Last Expedition*, vol. 1 (London: Smith, Elder, 1913), 417.

New York Times, March 8, 1912.

Barry Lopez, *Arctic Dreams: Imagination and Desire in a Northern Landscape* (New York: Charles Scribner's Sons, 1986).

Robert E. Peary, *The North Pole* (New York: Frederick A. Stokes, 1910), 288.

R. F. Scott, *The Voyage of the Discovery*, vol. 1 (London: Smith, Elder, 1905), 467–68.

Wilfred Thesiger, *The Life of My Choice* (New York: Norton, 1988).

Walter Wellman, "To the Pole by Airship," *Bur* 14 (March 1909): 42.

Epilogue: Final frontiers?

Jacques-Yves Cousteau and James Dugan, eds., *Captain Cousteau's Underwater Treasury* (New York: Harper, 1959), xv.

David Robertson, *George Mallory* (London: Faber, 1969), 116.

Further reading

General books on exploration

Buisseret, David, ed. *The Oxford Companion to World Exploration*. New York: Oxford University Press, 2007.

Fernández-Armesto, Felipe. *Pathfinders: A Global History of Exploration*. New York: W. W. Norton, 2006.

Hanbury-Tenison, Robin, ed. *The Great Explorers*. London: Thames and Hudson, 2010.

Kennedy, Dane, ed. *Reinterpreting Exploration: The West in the World*. New York: Oxford University Press, 2014.

Prehistoric/ancient exploration

Adams, Colin, and Ray Laurence, eds. *Travel and Geography in the Roman Empire*. London: Routledge, 2001.

Cunliffe, Barry. *The Extraordinary Voyage of Pytheas the Greek*. New York: Penguin, 2003.

Markoe, Glenn E. *Phoenicians*. Berkeley: University of California Press, 2000.

The Polynesians

Dening, Greg. *Beach Crossings: Voyaging Across Times, Cultures, and Self*. Philadelphia: University of Pennsylvania Press, 2004.

Irwin, Geoffrey. *The Prehistoric Exploration and Colonisation of the Pacific*. Cambridge: Cambridge University Press, 1994.

Jones, Terry L., et al. *Polynesians in America: Pre-Columbian contacts with the New World*. Lanham, MD: AltaMira Press, 2011.

Kirch, P. V. L. *On the Road of the Winds: An Archaeological History of the Pacific Islands Before European Contact*. Berkeley: University of California Press, 2000.

The Norse/Vikings

Ferguson, Robert. *The Vikings: A History*. New York: Penguin, 2009.

Fitzhugh, W. W., and E. I. Ward, eds. *Vikings: The North Atlantic Saga*. Washington, DC: Smithsonian Institution Press, 2000.

Seaver, Kirsten A. *The Last Vikings: The Epic Story of the Great Norse Voyagers*. London: I. B. Tauris, 2010.

Medieval exploration

Dunn, Ross E. *The Adventures of Ibn Battuta: A Muslim Traveller of the Fourteenth Century*. Berkeley: University of California Press, 2012.

Fernández-Armesto, Felipe. *Before Columbus: Exploration and Colonisation from the Mediterranean to the Atlantic, 1249-1492*. Basingstoke: Macmillan, 1987.

Larner, John. *Marco Polo and the Discovery of the World*. New Haven, CT: Yale University Press, 1999.

Mirsky, Jeannette, ed. *The Great Chinese Travellers*. Chicago: University of Chicago Press, 1974.

Phillips, J. K. S. *The Medieval Expansion of Europe*. Oxford: Oxford University Press, 1988.

The "Age of Exploration and Discovery"

Appleby, Joyce. *Shores of Knowledge: New World Discoveries and the Scientific Imagination*. New York: W. W. Norton, 2013.

Boyle, David. *Toward the Setting Sun: Columbus, Cabot, Vespucci, and the Race for America*. New York: Walker, 2008.

Casale, Giancarlo. *The Ottoman Age of Exploration*. New York: Oxford University Press, 2010.

Fernández-Armesto, Felipe. *Columbus*. Oxford: Oxford University Press, 1991.

Fernández-Armesto, Felipe. *1492: The Year the World Began*. New York: HarperOne, 2009.

Morison, Samuel Eliot. *The European Discovery of America*, 2 vols. New York: Oxford University Press, 1993.

Exploration and the Enlightenment

Carter, Paul. *The Road to Botany Bay: An Exploration of Landscape and History*. Chicago: University of Chicago Press, 1987.

Liebersohn, Harry. *The Travelers' World: Europe to the Pacific*. Cambridge, MA: Harvard University Press, 2006.

Livingstone, David N., and Charles W. J. Withers, eds. *Geography and Enlightenment*. Chicago: University of Chicago Press, 1999.

Safier, Neil. *Measuring the New World: Enlightenment Science and South America*. Chicago: University of Chicago Press, 2008.

Salmond, Anne. *The Trial of the Cannibal Dog: The Remarkable Story of Captain Cook's Encounters in the South Seas*. New Haven, CT: Yale University Press, 2003.

Thomas, Nicholas. *Cook: The Extraordinary Voyages of Captain James Cook*. New York: Walker, 2003.

Walls, Laura Dassow. *The Passage to Cosmos: Alexander Humboldt and the Shaping of America*. Chicago: University of Chicago Press, 2009.

North American exploration

Allen, John Logan, ed. *North American Exploration*, 3 vols. Lincoln: University of Nebraska Press, 1997.

Carter, Edward C. II. *Surveying the Record: North American Scientific Exploration to 1930*. Philadelphia: American Philosophical Society, 1999.

Frost, Orcutt. *Bering: The Russian Discovery of America*. New Haven, CT: Yale University Press, 2003.

Goetzmann, William H. *Exploration and Empire: The Explorer and the Scientist in the Winning of the American West*. New York: Alfred A. Knopf, 1966.

Goetzmann, William H. *New Lands, New Men: America and the Second Great Age of Discovery*. New York: Viking, 1986.

Sachs, Aaron. *The Humboldt Current: Nineteenth Century Exploration and the Roots of American Environmentalism*. New York: Viking, 2006.

Exploration and nineteenth-century empire

Bonhomme, Brian. *Russian Exploration, from Siberia to Space: A History*. Jefferson, NC: McFarland, 2012.

Driver, Felix. *Geography Militant: Cultures of Exploration and Empire*. Oxford: Blackwell, 2001.

Kennedy, Dane. *The Last Blank Spaces: Exploring Africa and Australia*. Cambridge, MA: Harvard University Press, 2013.

Pettitt, Clare. *Dr. Livingstone, I Presume? Missionaries, Journalists, Explorers, and Empire*. Cambridge, MA: Harvard University Press, 2007.

Ross, A. C. *David Livingstone: Mission and Empire*. London: Hambledon, 2002.

Stafford, Robert A. "Scientific Exploration and Empire." In *The Oxford History of the British Empire*, vol. 3, ed. Andrew Porter. Oxford: Oxford University Press, 1999.

Polar exploration

Barczewski, Stephanie. *Antarctic Destinies: Scott, Shackleton, and the Changing Face of Heroism*. London: Hambledon Continuum, 2007.

Larson, Edward J. *An Empire of Ice: Scott, Shackleton, and the Heroic Age of Antarctic Science*. New Haven, CT: Yale University Press, 2011.

McCannon, John. *A History of the Arctic: Nature, Exploration and Exploitation*. London: Reaktion Books, 2012.

Robinson, Michael F. *The Coldest Crucible: Arctic Exploration and American Culture*. Chicago: University of Chicago Press, 2006.

Solomon, Susan. *The Coldest March: Scott's Fatal Antarctic Expedition*. New Haven, CT: Yale University Press, 2001.

Oceans and outer space

Cousteau, Jacques-Yves. *The Silent World*. With Frédéric Dumas. New York: Harper, 1953.

Naylor, Simon, and James R. Ryan, eds. *New Spaces for Exploration: Geographies of Discovery in the Twentieth Century*. London: I. B. Tauris, 2010.

Pyne, Stephen J. *Voyager: Seeking Newer Worlds in the Third Great Age of Discovery*. New York: Viking, 2010.

Rozwadowski, Helen M. *Fathoming the Ocean: The Discovery and Exploration of the Deep Sea*. Cambridge, MA: Harvard University Press, 2008.

Index

Index